The Intelligent School

Barbara MacGilchrist, Kate Myers and
Jane Reed

P·C·P
Paul Chapman
Publishing Ltd

Paul Chapman Publishing Ltd
A SAGE Publications Company
6 Bonhill Street
London EC2A 4PU

British Library Cataloguing in Publication Data

MacGilchrist, Barbara
  The intelligent school
  1. School management and organization
  I. Title   II. Myers, Kate   III. Reed, Jane
  371.2

ISBN 1 85396 342 9

Typeset by Dorwyn Ltd., Rowlands Castle, Hants
Printed and bound by Athenaeum Press, Gateshead

E F G H   3 2 1 0

Contents

Foreword

This is a book for our time. Its purpose is to help practitioners to draw together some key findings from four areas of research that have relevance for every classroom in the country: school effectiveness, school improvement, learning and teaching. The book, however, does more than this. MacGilchrist, Myers and Reed are representatives of a new, and a very welcome, breed of educationalist. They have a solid background of senior positions in a variety of schools and local education authorities. To this sound foundation they have grafted research skills and knowledge of the field. They have thus combed the relevant literatures and synthesised a coherent account of improvement that should make sense to practitioners.

The new reality facing schools is that they have to improve but, unlike so much else that has been written recently about schools, the preferred solution put forward by MacGilchrist, Myers and Reed is school self-improvement. The debate about self-improvement often takes the form of an argument between two opposing groups. The *doves* argue that unless people do it for themselves, change will remain superficial. According to them, teachers can learn the required rules to achieve a reasonable Ofsted report but will only really challenge themselves and their practice if they can take ownership of standards. The *hawks*, meanwhile, argue that self-evaluation is likely to be soft-centred and that, without a hard-edged external probing, difficult questions and judgements will always be shirked.

These authors suggest a middle course through which school staff can adopt an active stance, learning good practice from elsewhere, using data and a rigour that will enable them to take charge of their own improvement. Of course, this process will involve them in concentrating on the positive and in building up confidence. The hawks may interpret this as complacency but teachers should not be put off. I have always found that the more confident people are the ones most able to accept criticism. In contrast, it is those that are insecure who build barriers to prevent the evaluation of their work.

The notion that heads and teachers can be active promoters of change may surprise some readers. We have grown too accustomed to seeing them oppressed by external changes, subject to unfair criticism and learning to rely totally on outside experts for evaluation. In this book, the authors show that there is an alternative and that it is much healthier for all of us – pupils and parents, teachers and our society.

The teaching profession began with untrained graduates working in the public schools and pupil monitors regurgitating the lessons just taught to them in the elementary schools. Only in recent years have the entry qualifications approached those commonly used in other professions. Not surprisingly, therefore, the tradition – so strong in other fields – of reading research reports is weak among teachers. Impressively this is growing as the number of senior staff enrolling in universities for higher degrees illustrates.

In their book the authors argue that the *'the intelligent school* is much more than the sum of its parts'. They identify nine intelligences they associate with this idea. Underpinning their views is the notion that schools are organic and dynamic institutions and that those working in them have the power and responsibility to take charge of their own destiny. This is fighting talk and it represents a new spirit emerging from both academics and practitioners. After years of being cowed, they are standing up and fighting for what they believe is important.

Books like *The Intelligent School* will encourage teachers to look to research for ideas and inspiration. The authors also set a high standard for others in universities to follow. They write clearly and directly. They also relate academic findings to practical experience. This bridging role is essential but, in my experience, difficult to do well. I congratulate MacGilchrist, Myers and Reed on their achievement. I hope all who read this exciting book will be encouraged to take up the responsibilities for improvement advocated here. If we, as a nation, are to improve learning and raise the average standards reached in schools and colleges, we need well-informed, highly skilled practitioners ready and willing to champion the mission of their school. They must turn the public debate from one of shame and blame to one in which a self-critical but confident pride can play a part.

Peter Mortimore
Institute of Education
March 1997

Acknowledgements

This book is dedicated to the teachers and pupils with whom we have had the privilege of working. It is the lessons they have taught us that have inspired us to write. Thanks go especially to all those who provided us with practical examples of their work, some of which we have incorporated into the book. We are also indebted to the many researchers on whose work we have drawn and to John MacBeath, Sue Purves and our colleagues at the Institute of Education: Caroline Gipps, Harvey Goldstein, Elizabeth Leo, Chris Watkins and, in particular, Peter Mortimore, and Louise Stoll who found the time to read and comment on early drafts. Special thanks and gratitude go to Karen Easton for her commitment, enthusiasm and support in ensuring that the book came to fruition.

Barbara MacGilchrist
Kate Myers
Jane Reed
1997

In times of change, learners inherit the earth, while the learned find themselves beautifully equipped to deal with a world that no longer exists.

(Hoffer)

Continuous learning – for everyone – is central to the notion of *the intelligent school.*

Introduction

The purpose of the book

This is a book for practitioners. It has been written for those who have the major responsibility for making schools work, namely classroom teachers and members of staff who have leadership and management responsibilities at whatever level and in whatever type of school. It is a book that may also be of interest to policy-makers and to those who work in a support role with schools. Our purpose in writing *The Intelligent School* is to offer a practical resource to schools to enable them to maximise their improvement efforts. Our aim is to help schools to be *intelligent* organisations; in other words, the type of school that can synthesise different kinds of knowledge, experience and ideas in order to be confident about current achievements and to have the ability to decide what to do next.

Three of us have written the book together. Between us we have more than 80 years experience of working in and with primary, secondary and special schools, local education authorities and academic institutions. The book grew out of a number of concerns that we found we shared:

- the need to recognise that there is no blueprint for improving schools, rather schools can be enabled to make intelligent, informed decisions about what is likely to work best for them;

- the need to focus school improvement efforts on the classroom;

- the need to make research findings more accessible and usable for teachers;

- the need to support practitioners in making better sense of what they are implicitly doing;

- the need to celebrate and disseminate some of the good practice already going on in schools across the country.

We have tried to distil and share some of the knowledge, experience and ideas we have gained from working with both academics and practitioners. We want to enable schools to become more familiar with relevant research and to ask the sorts of questions we often ask ourselves – 'What do these findings mean for us, particularly on a wet Friday afternoon. In what ways can we use them to help us to become more effective?' Our review of the research literature is by no means exhaustive. We have chosen research findings that we think are interesting and of considerable importance for practitioners. We have used practical examples provided by schools, local education authorities and education consultants to illustrate some of the different ways in which schools, often intuitively, have put some of the research theory into practice.

The three of us share a further concern. 'School improvement' has become the 'flavour of the month'. Unfortunately, the media interpretation of this trend, often encouraged by political pronouncements, has been that the majority of schools are failing and that drastic measures are needed to 'pull them up by their bootstraps'. This scenario does not match with our experience. We are agreed that, regrettably, there definitely are some schools that for a variety of reasons are seriously failing their pupils and that in such cases drastic measures are needed. However, as far as the majority of schools are concerned our experience is that headteachers and their staff are endeavouring to seek ways of continuously improving their effectiveness. As Hopkins, Ainscow and West (1994) have put it: 'You don't have to be ill to get better'.

Our experience also tells us that whilst some schools, because of their particular circumstances, are successful at improving themselves with limited external support, many schools are seeking help with their improvement efforts. Such an attitude has pluses and minuses. On the plus side, for example, it means that these schools are receptive to change and want to improve, both of which are important prerequisites for moving forward. On the negative side, however, this can encourage a dependency culture whereby schools seek blueprints or formulae that they can apply in a mechanistic way regardless of their own particular context and culture. This, in turn, encourages external consultants and agencies to offer simplistic solutions to what are often very complex issues.

Through our work as Associate Directors of the Institute of Education's International School Effectiveness and Improvement Centre (ISEIC), we are also only too well aware of the academic debates about the relationship between school effectiveness and school improvement research and about the dangers of simplistic interpretations of complex research findings. We share these concerns. We also consider that the findings of these two areas of research are not enough in themselves. We believe that *teaching and learning* are at the heart of school improvement. They are the core business of schools. Therefore, knowledge about the findings of research into both effective learning and effective teaching is also essential. We feel that for a school to work successfully it needs to be able to *put the pieces together* from these four areas of research in an *intelligent* way so as to see the connections between them and then to consider, in relation to its own context, the practical implications for the classroom and for the school as a whole.

This book attempts to address these shared concerns. It aims to inform practitioners of some of the key messages from these four interrelated areas of research and to illustrate, through the use of real examples, a variety of ways in which these findings can be pieced together in a practical way to improve teaching and learning.

To help us write this book, we wrote to schools and LEAs across the country seeking examples of their current practice. The schools and LEAs from which examples are drawn would be the first to add a disclaimer to the effect that these are not blueprints for all schools to follow. Where possible we have used the examples sent but, of course, are not advocating these as the way or, indeed, the only way to do things. We were determined, however, to include real examples because we believe that a major way of improving schools is to enable them to share and learn from one another's practice. The examples represent a spread of schools and LEAs although we were not surprised that more schools in the London area with whom the Institute works in close partnership in a variety of ways responded to our request for information.

Finally, we take a fresh look at schools as organisations and, building on our collective experience, we argue that 'putting the pieces together' of school effectiveness and school improvement with learning and teaching is not as simple as it sounds, nor as some people would have us believe. It is certainly not a mechanistic or linear activity. All important is the capacity a school has to use this knowledge. We draw on Gardner's (1983) notion of multiple intelligence and on recent thinking about the nature of organisations to offer a new way of looking at schools and their capacity to improve. We identify nine intelligences that when used in combination enable a school to have the capacity to achieve its goals successfully. We argue that: *'the intelligent school is greater than the sum of its parts'.* Through the use of its *'corporate intelligence'* it is in a powerful position to improve its effectiveness.

The structure of the book

In Chapter 1 we identify some of the important findings being disseminated from the school effectiveness and the school improvement literature. We emphasise the strengths and the limitations of these findings and argue that they must not be seen as an end in themselves or as sufficient to make schools work effectively. In Chapter 2 we reflect on the nature of learning. We begin with a consideration of some of the different theories about how we learn and about the purpose of learning. We then reflect on what it means to be a learner, the different ways in which learning can take place and on what learners themselves expect from those who teach and work with them. In Chapter 3 we turn our attention to sources of evidence concerned with the characteristics of effective teaching. We begin by asking the question: 'what do we mean by teaching?' We then consider three core dimensions of teacher effectiveness. These dimensions concern the knowledge, understanding and skills teachers need to have in relation to: the content of teaching; how pupils learn; and how to manage the process of learning and teaching in the classroom.

In the next two chapters we consider some of the practical ways in which schools can use, and indeed are using often implicitly, some of the findings from research into these four different aspects of schooling to maximise their improvement efforts. We do this from two perspectives:

- ways of supporting teachers' learning (Chapter 4)

- ways of tracking and evaluating pupils' progress and achievement (Chapter 5).

The focus of Chapter 4 is the professional development of teachers. We concentrate on some of the practical ways in which schools provide teachers with opportunities to learn with and from one another 'on the job' and from best practice elsewhere. We argue that teachers' learning and pupils' learning are inextricably linked. Chapter 5 addresses the issue of pupil progress and achievement from year to year. We examine some of the practical ways in which schools track and evaluate pupils' learning throughout their time in school. Three different types of evidence schools gather about pupils' progress and achievement are identified. How schools use this evidence to set specific targets for improvement is then illustrated. The chapter concludes with examples of how schools ensure that teaching and learning in the classroom are at the heart of their improvement efforts.

The last chapter concerns the school as a whole. The focus is on the title of the book – *The Intelligent School*. We draw together the themes developed in the previous chapters and translate these into nine different but interdependent intelligences. We describe the characteristics of these intelligences and argue that when they are used in combination they enable a school to apply the knowledge and skills it has to maximum effect in classrooms and across the school as a whole.

How the book can be used

Our intention is that *The Intelligent School* can be used by individual teachers, groups of teachers and whole-school staffs. The first three chapters provide the framework for the chapters that follow. The next two chapters concern a different aspect of school life, either of which could be used as a focus for improvement depending on the particular needs of a school. At the end of each of these chapters some questions for consideration are provided which offer an agenda for discussion and reflection. The questions can be used by individual teachers or as a catalyst for school-based inservice training sessions. The final chapter provides a framework for the staff as a group to examine their capacity for improvement. We have tried to formulate ideas and questions in such a way as to offer both a challenge and a support to schools in their efforts to make a real difference in terms of the quality of education they provide for their pupils.

1

Improving the effectiveness of schools

Educational change depends on what teachers do and think. It's as simple and as complex as that.

(Fullan, 1991, p. 117)

Lessons from school effectiveness literature

Making a difference to pupils' chances

Pupils only get one chance in the reception class, one time in year 9 and, in fact, only one chance each year. Time in school, therefore, is precious and for the pupils it cannot be repeated. The key message from the school effectiveness literature is that schools can make a difference for the better (Edmonds, 1979; Rutter *et al.*, 1979; Mortimore *et al.*, 1988) or even for the worse (Myers, 1995). This is a very powerful message, probably the most powerful that has come from this area of literature. It both empowers and challenges practitioners, bestowing the possibility of making a difference to the life chances of children alongside giving the responsibility for doing so.

The challenge is real because research findings demonstrate that some schools can make much more of a difference than others and that schools serving very similar intakes can give their pupils very different experiences and achieve different outcomes for their pupils.

In the literature, an effective school has been described as 'one in which pupils progress further than might be expected from consideration of its intake' (Mortimore, 1991, p. 9), and one which 'adds extra value to its students' outcomes in comparison with other schools serving similar intakes' (Sammons, Hillman and Mortimore, 1995, p. 3).

Adding value for pupils

These definitions have helped us to focus on individual pupils' *progress* as well as the *outcomes* of their learning. Hence the emergence of the concept of 'value-added' which is embedded within these definitions. This concept has made a significant impact on schools, particularly in helping staff realise the need to track and monitor pupil progress and not just concentrate on outcomes. This has led to *intelligent* schools developing a range of strategies to monitor progress including the systematic collection of data to provide the necessary evidence of improvement. For example, in primary schools it has resulted in an increasing acceptance of the need to gather base-line data on children when they first begin school, so as to be able to support and monitor their progress.

We welcome these moves, but value-added is a complex concept. Like many of our colleagues, we would like to urge caution in using and interpreting such data, not least because of the use or not of value-added information to publish league tables of school results. It is important to remember that raw results describe the grades or levels that pupils have obtained. They do not describe how well a school has performed. It is only through the use of value-added results that it is possible to demonstrate how effective a school is in promoting pupils' achievement. However, even these results need to have a 'health warning' attached to them. They may, for example, mask a high turnover of pupils (Goldstein, 1996). Also, because of the limited number of pupils normally included in the sample, there are inherent limitations built into the technique when using it to make comparisons between schools. This means that whilst the technique of value-added can be used as a screening device to identify very low performing or very high performing schools, it is not able to provide finely graded differences between schools (Goldstein and Spiegelhalter, 1996).

Using value-added data is most useful for helping individual schools to pinpoint areas of good practice and aspects of school life that need to be improved. When using value-added data, however, there are a number of issues that schools need to consider. The technique enables a school to take account of 'givens' that may have an impact on pupil outcomes such as prior attainment, socio-economic status, gender and ethnicity. It is therefore important that these pupil intake factors are built into the equation. In this way it is possible to use the information gained on individual pupils as an internal screening device.

Value-added data can also be used as a screening device to identify individual pupils whose 'predicted' or 'expected' achievements are very different from those observed. For this to work, however, it is pupils' achievements *during* their time in school, for example at the end of a year, not their final end results which are crucial. This implies a different data collection strategy but one which is potentially more useful than comparisons of whole institutions. Pupils who depart markedly from their expected levels of achievement can be identified and, if necessary, can become a focus for additional support.

It must be remembered, however, that even at an individual pupil level, the reliability of the screening instrument being used will need to be taken into account when assessing a pupil's potential or actual performance. Also, different instruments need to be used in order to assess a range of pupil outcomes. It is important to do this because research evidence indicates that pupils can achieve very differently depending on the outcomes being measured (Mortimore, Sammons and Thomas, 1994). For example, a pupil's attainment may be very high but her or his self-image and attitude to school may be very low. Such a finding signals the necessity to develop a range of pupil 'measures' to provide a much fuller picture of a school's effectiveness.

Differential effectiveness in relation to groups of pupils and specific subjects and departments can also be assessed using value-added data. Again, this is important because research has shown that, whilst on the surface a school's overall results may look impressive, this snapshot of attainment may well mask noticeable differences in outcomes for specific groups of pupils and subject areas (O'Donoghue *et al.*, 1997, Sammons, Thomas and Mortimore, 1997). As with individual pupil data, it is necessary to look at results over several years to be able to make a more reliable judgement about the stability and continuity of the trends emerging. It is also necessary to bear in mind the margin of error or uncertainty that can be associated with such results if small numbers of pupils are involved (Goldstein, 1996).

Measuring what we value

A report from the USA called *Education Counts* (1991) states that we must learn to measure what we value rather than value what we can easily measure. One of the limitations of school effectiveness research is that it is comparatively easy to track progress and assess value-added by using statistical data such as base-line scores and examination results. Assessing the effectiveness of a school, therefore, has often been based on a narrow set of quantitative measures. For example, reading and mathematics tests results in the primary school are used because of the ready availability of standardised tests in these areas of the curriculum. Using qualitative measures is methodologically much more difficult. Peter Mortimore and colleagues were amongst the first researchers to attempt to combine different types of measures to assess the effectiveness of schools. In the Junior School study (Mortimore *et al.*, 1988), as well as testing children's reading, writing, speaking and mathematical skills, their attendance, self-image, behaviour and attitudes towards different types of school activities were also measured. Other researchers have attempted to develop qualitative indicators. Gray (1995) argues that the effectiveness of schools can best be judged by academic progress, pupil satisfaction and pupil–teacher relationships. John MacBeath and colleagues (1992) have developed ethos indicators for the Scottish school system. The main message from all these studies is the danger of concentrating on too narrow a definition of achievement when assessing a school's effectiveness.

Defining achievement

We believe it is essential for schools to have a broad definition of achievement. David Hargreaves and colleagues (ILEA, 1984) suggested that there are at least four aspects of achievement that a school needs to develop:

- Dealing with the capacity to remember and use facts. This aspect concerns the type of achievement that public examinations tend to measure. It emphasises a pupil's ability to memorise and reproduce knowledge often in a written form.

- Practical and spoken skills. This aspect concerns the practical capacity to apply knowledge with an emphasis on problem-solving and investigational skills.

- Personal and social skills. The focus here is on a pupil's capacity to communicate with and relate to others. It also concerns personal characteristics such as initiative, self-reliance and leadership potential.

- Motivation and self-confidence. This concerns a pupil's self-image and ability, for example, to persevere in the face of failure.

Howard Gardner (1983) working in the USA has suggested that people have more than one intelligence. He believes that there are at least seven intelligences which each of us has the capacity to develop. Similarly, Daniel Goleman (1996) emphasises the importance of emotional intelligence. We describe these intelligences and comment on them in more detail in Chapter 2.

These views and findings of researchers provide a challenge for practitioners especially when there are disagreements nationally amongst policy-makers about the purpose of education and, therefore, the content of the curriculum. This lack of agreement about the aims of education makes it even more important for each school to be quite clear what its aims are and, therefore, the criteria the headteacher and staff will use to assess their own effectiveness.

The characteristics of effective schools

Having a clear set of agreed aims has been identified as one of the characteristics of an effective school. The identification of such characteristics has been another major contribution from this area of research. There are some who would argue that many of the characteristics are obvious, so why make so much of them? This is a good example of the value of research as often it does confirm what practitioners might say is no more than common sense. But, of course, what is seen as common sense by one group might be viewed very differently by another – witness, for example, the ongoing debate about the teaching of reading. The important message about the characteristics of effective schools, in terms of the definitions given earlier, is that from the information we have there appear to be a number of characteristics that, when present, make a difference to the life chances of the pupils in that school.

Pam Sammons and two other colleagues were recently commissioned by the Office for Standards in Education (Ofsted) to undertake a review of international school effectiveness literature, particularly from the United Kingdom, North America and the Netherlands. They were asked to assess whether or not, despite the many differences in approaches to education from one country to the next, it was possible to find distinctive features that successful schools have in common. The review confirmed that there appear to be at least eleven characteristics that are present in those schools that do add value for their pupils. Table 1.1 reproduces the synopsis provided in the write-up of this literature review (Sammons, Hillman and Mortimore, 1995, p. 8).

For the purposes of this book we saw no point in providing a description of each of these characteristics because they are well known and readily available for practitioners to read about. However, we do want to reflect on these characteristics because we believe that by developing them schools will become more effective. We asked ourselves two questions:

- Are they all of equal value or are some more central than others?
- How can a school develop these characteristics?

When considering the first question we turned our thoughts back to Howard Gardner. We wondered if the presence of these characteristics means that schools themselves need to develop different kinds of intelligence to function effectively. We return to this question in Chapter 6. We also drew on research literature about the nature of organisations beyond the world of education and again we will return to this literature in the final chapter.

Table 1.1 Eleven characteristics found in effective schools

1	**Professional leadership**	Firm and purposeful
		A participative approach
		The leading professional
2	**Shared vision and goals**	Unity of purpose
		Consistency of practice
		Collegiality and collaboration
3	**A learning environment**	An orderly atmosphere
		An attractive working environment
4	**Concentration on teaching and learning**	Maximisation of learning time
		Academic emphasis
		Focus on achievement
5	**Purposeful teaching**	Efficient organisation
		Clarity of purpose
		Structured lessons
		Adaptive practice
6	**High expectations**	High expectations all round
		Communicating expectations
		Providing intellectual challenge
7	**Positive reinforcement**	Clear and fair discipline
		Feedback
8	**Monitoring progress**	Monitoring pupil performance
		Evaluating school performance
9	**Pupil rights and responsibilities**	Raising pupil self-esteem
		Positions of responsibility
		Control of work
10	**Home–school partnership**	Parental involvement in their children's learning
11	**A learning organisation**	School-based staff development

Source: Sammons, Hillman and Mortimore 1995, p. 8

These reflections, coupled with our own knowledge and experience, led us to the conclusion that the characteristics are not of equal value although they are all important. We would argue that there appear to be some core essential characteristics and that if these are not present then the other characteristics are unlikely to be present either and even if some of them are, they will be operating in a vacuum. In other words, we believe that some characteristics are of central importance and that the remaining ones arise out of or are *nested* within them. From our experience we would argue that the three essential core characteristics of an effective school are:

- professional high quality leadership and management (we have added management because, as discussed later in the chapter, we believe both are essential);
- a concentration on teaching and (pupil) learning;

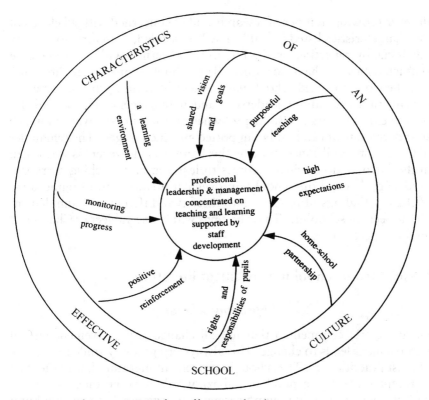

Figure 1.1 Characteristics of an effective school
© 1997 B. MacGilchrist, K. Myers, and J. Reed

- a learning organisation, i.e. a school with staff who are willing to be learners and to participate in a staff development programme.

Our experience is that schools that have these characteristics are able to create the right conditions to enable them to develop into very effective institutions in terms of their pupils' progress and outcomes. The result is a school that develops the kind of culture as expressed through the remaining eight characteristics listed in the Sammons, Hillman and Mortimore study. Figure 1.1 illustrates what we mean.

We have tried to create a dynamic diagram as opposed to a static one because schools are ever-changing, organic institutions. We believe that *the intelligent school* is able to bring these core and related characteristics together to provide a coherent experience for pupils in each classroom, department and the school as a whole.

To seek the answer to the second question – how can a school develop these characteristics to become more effective? – it is necessary to go beyond the school effectiveness literature. We are only too well aware of the ever-growing number of research studies concerned with all eleven of the characteristics listed in Table 1.1. We decided, therefore, to narrow our focus by reflecting on the literature concerned with the three core characteristics we have identified. The school improvement literature and the closely related school management literature provide some important messages about leadership and management. The school improvement literature is also helpful when considering the ways in which staff development can best be supported and encouraged. The remainder of this chapter will concentrate on this literature. However, as we argued in the Introduction, when it comes to learning and teaching there is a need to go beyond the school improvement literature to examine some of the key findings of research into these two different but complementary aspects of schooling. These findings will be the subject of Chapters 2 and 3 respectively.

Lessons from school improvement literature

Improving schools

Fullan (1991) commented that not all change is improvement but all improvement leads to change. This always brings a wry smile to the face of most practitioners. The school improvement literature has burgeoned in recent years and a number of buzz words have become associated with it – vision, mission, empowerment, collegiality . . . to name but a few. Digging below the surface of this jargon some important messages for practitioners can be found. They are messages that have emerged as a result of researchers acting rather like 'flies on the wall' and observing and analysing practice in schools which are particularly successful at improving themselves.

What is school improvement?

Back in 1985 the 14 countries involved in an international school improvement project agreed the following definition of school improvement:

> A systematic, sustained effort aimed at change in learning conditions and other related conditions in one or more schools with the ultimate aim of accomplishing educational goals more effectively.
>
> (van Velzen *et al.*, 1985, p. 34)

More recently, Hopkins, Ainscow and West (1994, p. 3) have defined school improvement as:

> A distinct approach to educational change that enhances student outcomes as well as strengthening the school's capacity for managing change.

This definition emphasises the importance of assessing the outcomes of improvement efforts for the pupils themselves. In other words, the need to create a much closer link between school-wide improvements and improvements in the classroom.

Some key messages

The literature makes it quite clear that there is no set recipe for achieving improvement. What *the intelligent school* has been able to do, however, is to maximise its improvement efforts by heeding some of the key messages that have emerged from this area of research. We have chosen to concentrate on six interrelated messages as we believe they are particularly helpful for schools:

● change takes time

● a school's capacity for change will vary

● change is complex

● change needs to be well led and managed

● teachers need to be the main agents of change

● the pupils need to be the main focus for change.

Change takes time

A superficial quick fix approach to change may end up being no more than moving the deckchairs around on the Titanic (Stoll and Fink, 1996). If a school is serious about wanting to improve learning conditions and, ultimately, the standards of achievement of the pupils then this requires a systematic, sustained effort as suggested in the van Velzen definition. Yet, as the opening two sentences of this chapter reminded us, time is precious for pupils and if a school needs to improve then it has a responsibility to its pupils to make the necessary changes as soon as possible. This is the challenge for schools – how to bring about change (improvement) as soon as possible but in such a way as to ensure that the improvements are for the better and can be sustained. This fits in with the findings of Goldstein and Thomas (1995) that to assess the effectiveness of a school in terms of value-added you need at least three years' worth of data to be able to make a judgement as to whether or not a school's performance is improving.

Michael Fullan (1992), one of the gurus of the change literature, recognises this dilemma and encourages schools to 'ready, fire, aim'. His basic message is that change can be messy, that it is difficult to predict exactly how things will go and that rarely does the end result turn out as planned. He is of the view that it is better to get started and then modify and adjust as you go. This reflects the reality facing schools. However, Fullan and other researchers (Hargreaves and Hopkins, 1991; West and Ainscow, 1991) do subscribe to the van Velzen view that improvement requires a sustained effort. Louis and Miles (1992), who did an interesting study of six urban high schools in the USA, introduced the concept of 'evolutionary' planning. They argued that schools need a planned approach to change that is flexible and adaptable rather than rigidly imposed. In other words, a planned approach to change that is long-term and flexible so that, as circumstances change, modifications can be made and unexpected events catered for. We argue in the final chapter that this is a characteristic of *the intelligent school*.

Throughout the United Kingdom and in many other countries worldwide – for example, Canada, Australia and New Zealand – school development planning has been adopted to achieve this kind of evolutionary approach to planning. There appears to be a general consensus that development planning is a strategy for school improvement. However, as the findings of a recent study of the impact of school development plans (MacGilchrist *et al.*, 1995) revealed, not all plans lead to improvement – more of this later.

An individual school's capacity for change varies

No two schools are the same. This is an obvious statement but worth emphasising. In their anxiety to improve the system, policy-makers have a tendency to forget this fact. All three of the authors of this book have been inspectors and advisers. We know from our personal experience that it is one thing to create a policy aimed at improving schools, it is quite another to ensure that all the schools in a district have the capacity to bring about these changes. It is no different for headteachers and their senior management teams. They know, only too well, that sense of frustration when a policy, seemingly agreed by the staff, fails to get put into practice for all kinds of reasons.

The message in the literature, therefore, is that schools cannot be treated as an homogeneous group. Each school's history and context will vary (Reynolds *et al.*, 1996). There will be some factors, be they internal or external ones, that are simply beyond a school's control such as its building, its geographical location and new legislation imposed from outside. There will be other factors that are within the control of the school to do something about, such as the type of leadership and management arrangements in place, the type of support provided for staff and the teaching methods used.

One of the most powerful messages to come out of the school improvement literature is the importance of a school's culture in relation to change. The culture of a school is seen as the deciding factor when it comes to a school's state of readiness and its capacity to improve. Those who study school improvement stress the importance of identifying the different cultures and subcultures within schools and that understanding a particular school's culture is a vital part of school improvement (Stoll and Fink, 1996). Defining the culture of a school is not easy. It has been called 'the way we do things around here' (Deal, 1987, p. 17). MacGilchrist *et al.*, (1995, p. 40) argue that 'the culture of an organisation is demonstrated through the ways in which those who belong to the organisation feel, think and act'. The authors identify three interrelated ways in which the culture of a school is expressed in practice:

- Professional relationships. For example, how headteachers and staff relate to and work with one another, their attitudes towards the pupils and others connected with the school and the quality of leadership and shared sense of purpose in respect of the school's aims.

- Organisational arrangements. For example, people management arrangements in respect of roles and responsibilities, procedures for making decisions, communication systems, pupil grouping and pastoral care along with environmental management arrangements such as the upkeep of the building and playground and the display of pupils' work in classrooms and the public areas of the school.

- Opportunities for learning – for both pupils and adults. For example, for pupils, the curriculum on offer, attitudes and expectations about what it is possible for pupils to achieve, equal opportunities concerns and the type of provision for special educational needs. For teachers, their own professional development and their attitude towards their own learning.

The authors concluded that:

These three dimensions are a practical manifestation of the underlying beliefs and values of a school community. All three are amenable to change so that, not only are they an expression of the present culture, but they can also help shape and change the future culture of the school.

(Ibid., p. 42).

The findings of Susan Rosenholtz's (1989) study of Tennessee schools and school districts illustrates these dimensions in practice. She found that the schools in her study tended to fall into two broad categories, 'moving' and 'stuck' schools. Needless to say, it was the moving schools that were successful in improving themselves. They were characterised by shared goals and teachers who were willing to collaborate with one another and who accepted that they still had things to learn whilst at the same time demonstrating a sense of confidence and commitment in what they were already doing. Susan Rosenholtz found there to be a relationship between this type of culture and improvements in pupils' learning.

The nine intelligences that we identify in Chapter 6 build on and develop the notion of the relationship between a school's culture and its capacity for improvement.

Change is complex

Again, this finding smacks of common sense but needs to be emphasised. An acceptance of the fact that change is complex is both a reassurance and a challenge for practitioners. Interpersonal relationships and micropolitics cannot be ignored when people and change are concerned. The prospect of change can mean different things to different people and, of course, people may react differently depending on the nature of the change being proposed. For example, some people find change exciting and that it sets the adrenaline flowing. Others may take a much more cynical view and think that if they keep their heads down then the latest idea will die a natural death. For others the prospect of change may be threatening. They may feel de-skilled and dislike dealing with uncertainty. These are all natural human reactions. What the literature tells us, however, is that real change – real improvement – is more than likely to be associated with some pain and some conflict, especially if it is challenging a person's fundamental beliefs and attitudes. Michael Fullan (1991) describes at least three different ways in which change can take place simultaneously by introducing new:

- equipment and materials (for example, the introduction of a new mathematics scheme)
- behaviours and practices (for example, a change in the way in which pupils are grouped for mathematics)
- beliefs and attitudes (for example, changing the way in which mathematics is taught).

(*our examples*)

Simply changing the first two without dealing with the third can lead to shallow, short-lived improvements (Cuban, 1988).

Change is also complex because it is not linear or mechanistic. It often happens in unpredictable and sometimes unlikely ways. This accords with new thinking about the nature of organisationsal change and development and we elaborate on this issue in the last chapter.

Another complex issue to emerge in the literature is the need to distinguish between means and ends (MacGilchrist, 1996). Originally, the emphasis of school improvement studies, as exemplified in the van Velzen definition, was on concentrating on improving general learning conditions within the school. Particular emphasis was placed on the importance of staff development. More recently, Fullan, Bennett and Rolheiser-Bennett (1990) have stressed the need to create a link between school-wide development, staff development and classroom development. The findings of the school development planning study in which one of us was involved illustrate the importance of this warning. The study (MacGilchrist *et al.*, 1995) found that there was only one type of plan that brought about improvements at these three levels. It was the type of plan that was well led and managed, had teacher development built in and, most importantly, had as its focus pupil progress and achievement in the classroom. In other words, school-wide improvements and the staff development programme were ultimately seen as a means to an end. More will be said about this in the final section in this chapter.

Change needs to be well led and managed

When writing about school development planning, Hargreaves and Hopkins (1991) stated that it is one thing to establish a plan for improvement, it is quite another to ensure that the plan is put into practice. They talked about the dangers of assuming that planned action will run on 'auto-pilot'.

In the literature a clear distinction is made between *leadership* and *management*. This distinction is illustrated by the definitions in Table 1.2. Schein (1985, p. 171) sums up the relationship between the two by stating that 'Both culture and structure, leadership and management are necessary if an organisation is to become highly effective'.

Table 1.2   Distinctions between leadership and management

Leadership	Management
'Building and maintaining an organisational culture' (Schein, 1985)	'Building and maintaining an organisational structure' (Schein, 1985)
'Establishing a mission for the school, giving a sense of direction' (Louis and Miles, 1992)	'Designing and carrying out plans, getting things done, working effectively with people' (Louis and Miles, 1992)
'Doing the right thing' (Bennis and Nanus, 1985)	'Doing things right' (Bennis and Nanus, 1985)

Southworth (1995) argues that traditional views about leadership and management are still prevalent particularly in primary schools. Leadership tends to be equated with the role of the headteacher who is deemed to be responsible for establishing the overall aims and purposes of the school and for managing the school with the help of the senior management team. School management is often still perceived as something that happens outside classrooms and to be concerned with systems and procedures often of a hierarchical nature.

Fullan (1992) argues for the need for a significant change in views about the role and purpose of leadership. He draws on the work of those who have studied organisations outside the world of education. For example, Block (1987) argues that organisations need to become much less bureaucratic and hierarchical because bureaucratic organisations encourage staff to look to 'managers' to provide the ideas. They discourage personal initiative and responsibility. He urges a move towards organisations that are led and managed in such a way as to enable staff to play an active part in shaping and improving the organisation. In this way, staff are encouraged to learn and develop as practitioners. Bennis and Nanus (1985) studied ninety top successful industrial leaders. They found that all of them were open to learning themselves and, likewise, encouraged and stimulated their staff to learn as well. The culture they fostered was one of trust and good communications about the aims of the organisation and the staff in these organisations were responsible and accountable for change.

Charles Handy (1984) studies schools from the perspective of an industrial management specialist. He has identified four types of school culture. There is the personal, informal *club* culture which revolves around a headteacher who has a network of power which is likened to a spider's web. There is the *role* culture which signifies a hierarchical role system which has formal procedures for managing the organisation. Such an organisation is managed rather then led by the headteacher and can be resistant to change. In contrast, there is the *task* culture which is responsive to change in a less individualistic way than a club culture. It is built around co-operative, not hierarchical, groups, and is usually a warm, friendly and forward-looking culture. Finally, there is the *person* culture which is a very individualistic one. The organisation is used by each member as a resource for developing their talents rather like stars loosely grouped in a constellation.

Handy found aspects of all four cultural types present in any one school and found, from his study, that no two schools were the same. He argues that the headteacher and senior management team need to be aware of these different types of culture and to use the strengths of each when appropriate. He believes that if schools are to improve, headteachers and their staff need to rethink their approach to leadership and management. He supports the traditional primary school philosophy of an emphasis on teaching pupils, rather than school subjects, and suggests that classroom teachers be valued as managers of learning.

Hargreaves and Hopkins (1991, p. 15) subscribe to Handy's view about management. They argue that: 'Management is about people. Management arrangements are what empower people. Empowerment is the purpose of management.' They criticise definitions of management that focus on structures and procedures. They point out that this can lead to a false divide between teaching and managing and can perpetuate the notion that 'managers manage and teachers teach'. In other words, teachers are also managers and, at the end of the day, the management of teaching and learning in the classroom is *the* most important management activity that goes on in school. We would argue too, that in *the intelligent school* senior managers see themselves as teachers and learners and as such provide a model for classroom teachers. Roland Barth (1990), for example, advocates that the headteacher should be the head learner.

Fullan (1992) argues for the need for leadership to be shared across a school and stresses the importance of the development of a professional culture in schools. This kind of culture is one in which there is an openness to new ideas. Staff give and receive help from one another and there is a sense of teamwork which has as its focus improving teaching and learning in the classroom. He sees this as both a strategy and an outcome of leadership and management. Such a view finds much support in the literature.

Teachers need to be the main agents of change

Like schools, teachers cannot be treated as a homogeneous group. The staff will be made up of a number of individuals who will bring to any proposed change different skills, knowledge and attitudes depending on their previous experience, their length of time in the school, their status within the school and their own particular concerns and interests, not least in terms of the stage they have reached in their own career as a teacher. There has been some interesting research into teachers' life histories and the changing values and attitudes that teachers have as they move through their career (Huberman, 1988; Sikes, 1992). These studies are a useful reminder for those with leadership and management responsibilities because, as Fullan (1991, p. 117) says, 'Educational change depends on what teachers do and think. It's as simple and as complex at that'.

The challenge for headteachers and their senior management teams is to find ways of bringing the staff on board and getting them committed to and prepared to become involved in change. All three of us have had experience of working with schools on a range of school improvement programmes. Nine times out of ten, the biggest hurdle to be overcome is achieving staff commitment to the change. Without it, long-lasting improvement will not occur.

As far as teachers are concerned, some important messages have come out of the school improvement literature. Good quality, professional working relationships are essential (Nias, Southworth and Yeomans 1989; Bolam *et al.*, 1993), so too are teamwork (Mortimore and Mortimore, 1991), shared leadership (Chrispeels, 1992; Louis and Miles, 1992) and shared understandings (Rosenholtz, 1989). A further key message is to do with teachers' own learning. Studies of schools and of other types of institutions beyond the world of education (Peters and Waterman, 1982) stress the importance of the attitude of the staff within such institutions towards their own learning and the priority given to staff development. Many studies have demonstrated the relationship between teachers' learning and school improvement (Rosenholtz, 1989; Chrispeels, 1992; Nias, Southworth and Campbell, 1992). Strategies for improving staff development programmes have been identified (Joyce and Showers, 1988; Hopkins, Ainscow and West, 1994) as have strategies for encouraging teachers to be more reflective and analytical (Joyce, 1991) and to gain greater control over the change programme themselves (Fink and Stoll, in press). In Chapter 4 we describe in detail practical ways for supporting teachers' learning.

As noted earlier, change can challenge teachers' fundamental beliefs and attitudes and lead to some form of conflict. It is essential that this healthy sign that change is taking place, is well led and managed. Understandably, teachers' main concerns are focused on what goes on in the classroom. The vast majority of teachers are hard-working, hard-pressed professionals for whom time is a precious commodity and mainly consumed in planning and preparing lessons, marking pupils' work and recording and assessing their progress. It is hardly surprising, therefore, that teachers often have a healthy scepticism towards change particularly if 'the management' or 'external agencies' are seen as the sole initiators of change which, in turn, is likely to result in a further increase in work-load for teachers. Our experience is that school improvement efforts that concentrate on the classroom in such a way that teachers experience the benefits of change for themselves and their children are the ones much more likely to be successful (MacGilchrist, 1996).

The pupils need to be the main focus for change

The findings of the study into the impact of development planning (MacGilchrist *et al.*, 1995) brought home the importance of schools having pupils' learning as the main focus for improvement. Of the four different types of plans, the authors found that only one made a real difference for children. A particularly poignant message from this research was that the type of development plan found in the majority of schools in the study – the co-operative plan – had many of the characteristics identified in the school effectiveness and school improvement literature. There was a willingness on behalf of the staff to work on school-wide improvements, although not all the staff had a 'piece of the action'. There was strong leadership from the headteacher. The senior management team managed the implementation of the plan very well. Resources were allocated to the priorities for improvement chosen. There was a detailed staff development programme directly linked with the school plan. However, although it was possible to identify improvements for the school as a whole such as new policy documents and changes in management practices, along with improvements in teachers' own professional development, it was not possible to track these improvements into the classroom for pupils. In other words, it was not possible to find examples of improved learning opportunities for them.

There was only one type of plan – the *corporate* plan – that did make an impact on pupils' learning. The reason for this was that whilst the plan had many of the characteristics of the co-operative plan, it had four vital additional ones. The leadership of the improvement efforts was shared amongst a number of teachers. Every member of staff had some piece of the action – something within the plan for improvement for which they had specific responsibility. The main focus for the plan was pupils' learning – their progress and achievement. Finally, strategies for monitoring and evaluating the impact of the plan and for providing data to establish further priorities for improvement were well developed.

Conclusion

The findings of this study are a good example of the ways in which much closer connections are now being made between the school effectiveness and school improvement literature – connections that have been long overdue (Reynolds, Hopkins and Stoll, 1993). As Chrispeels (1992, p. 167) says, 'It is no accident that monitoring of student progress and academic focus are two key features of effective schools.' We believe that whilst teachers' own learning is an important condition for school improvement, it cannot take place in a vacuum. It needs to be rooted in improving teaching and learning practices in the classroom. For such roots to take hold so that they result in real growth for adults and pupils alike, the headteacher and senior management team need to put in place school-wide support systems that provide the kinds of conditions in which teachers can maximise their efforts in the classroom. These conditions need to take account of the nature of learning which we reflect on in the next chapter.

Questions for discussion

1. How effective is your school? Is it equally effective for all groups of pupils? How do you find out?

2. How do you rate your school on the effectiveness characteristics, particularly the core ones we have identified?

3. What data (evidence) do you use to support, monitor and assess pupil progress and achievement? How useful and how accurate are these data?

4. How do your school improvement efforts enable a link to be made between school-wide development, teacher development and classroom practice?

5. How do you know your school improvement efforts are making a difference for pupils?

2

Learning from learning

Learning . . . that reflective activity which enables the learner to draw upon previous experience to understand and evaluate the present, so as to shape future action and formulate new knowledge.

(Abbott, 1994, p. viii)

What do we mean by learning?

Learning: knowledge acquired by study

(Oxford Dictionary, 1991)

This definition of learning is rather narrow. It either requires a wide definition of 'study' or excludes much learning, for example, the way babies and young children learn. Learning therefore, as implied in the discussion about achievement in Chapter 1, is much more than the acquisition of facts. It involves questioning, understanding, making connections between existing and new information, and subsequently, being able to make use of this new 'processed' information. It also involves the development of personal and social skills and is dependent in many respects upon the feelings, motivation and self-confidence of the person concerned.

Schools exist to enhance learning. Human beings have an innate capacity for learning that schools can enrich. They can also limit or damage it. Learning is a continuous process which starts before we arrive at school and which continues throughout our lives. The belief that *everyone* can learn, including profoundly disabled people, is becoming increasingly accepted in this country.

Teachers have always been aware that learning takes place in different settings and in different ways. In the school context it can take place in the classroom, in assembly, in the playground, in the toilets, in the corridors and in the staffroom. Whilst the school is not the only player in the learning process, it is a very important one and teachers have a vital role to contribute in helping their pupils' learning to be enhanced and effective.

For the purposes of this book we concentrate on the planned learning that takes place between teachers and pupils in school. We suggest that such learning often involves an unspoken, unwritten and sometimes unconscious *pact* between teacher and learner. For school learning to be enhanced and effective we argue that teachers need to understand the different factors that can influence a pupil's motivation and ability to learn. To do this teachers need to be:

- knowledgeable about learning as a process
- knowledgeable about learners and
- knowledgeable about what learners want.

Learners themselves also have a vital role to play in this process. In this chapter, we reflect on these three themes and on some of the implications for teachers in the classroom.

Learning as a process

Theories about how we learn

All areas of knowledge invent their own language which can be offputting and excluding for outsiders but useful for conveying new ideas precisely. 'Jargon' commonly used by those who study the theory of learning includes terms such as *calibration, scaffolding, zone of proximal development (ZPD), metacognition* and *accelerated learning.* In the next section we explore some of the research behind these terms because we believe it has relevance for practitioners.

There are many theories about learning. If we were to polarise them, on one extreme of the continuum is the 'traditional' model which views learning as the reception of knowledge, the learner as passive and the appropriate learning style as formal. The learner is seen as the 'empty vessel' and the teacher as the one responsible for filling this vessel. The passive learner responds to stimuli provided by the teacher. Learning is seen as linear and sequential. Little account is taken of what the learner may bring to the experience in the way of existing knowledge, existing language, self-esteem, previous experience of learning and preferred learning styles. On the other end of this continuum is the 'progressive' model which sees learning as discovery, the learner as active and the learning style as informal. The learner is fresh and innocent with time to experiment and has the desire and capacity to learn, perhaps with some judicious facilitation pointing her or him in the right direction.

Of course, this caricature is unfair to both theories and begs many questions, in particular, what it is that is being learnt and how important this is. For example, a different model may be appropriate when learning keyboard skills from that appropriate for learning Keynesian economics.

A widely held and current view is that learners learn through a process of first being exposed to new knowledge, and then attempting to make sense of the new knowledge in terms of their existing knowledge. Learners do this with other things (books, computers) and with other people (each other, their teacher). Learning thus can have an important interactive social component.

Cooper and McIntyre (1996) explain this process of making sense of new knowledge, known as *calibration*, in which the learner has an active role to play. Calibration involves the learner using the teacher's explanation to make her own sense of it and internalising the information in a way that is meaningful to her. The teacher's role in this transaction is to create circumstances for this to happen and, indeed, to make the learner want to participate in this process. To do this, the teacher has to diagnose and understand what stage the learner is at and provide the appropriate frame of reference or structure for her to move on. This process is sometimes described as *scaffolding*.

> The teacher provides model structures that enable the pupil to apply existing skills in new ways in the appropriation of new knowledge . . . The important point here, however, is that for scaffolding to be effective, the structure that is supplied by the teacher must be selected on the basis of its goodness of fit with the pupil's existing knowledge and cognitive structures.
>
> (Cooper and McIntyre, 1996, p. 97)

This is a challenge for teachers. If the new knowledge is too far removed from the learner's current understanding then it is likely that the learner will 'switch off' because she is unable to make sense of it. Piaget (1932) argues that the extent to which a learner can assimilate and accommodate new knowledge is dependent upon the stage of development the learner has reached. For Piaget the teacher has to be aware of the stage of development the learner is at in order to facilitate the learner reaching the next stage.

Vygotsky (1987) believes that learning and development are an inextricable part of the same process. The two concepts are not mutually exclusive. The teacher does not have to wait for the right developmental stage to be reached, but has to provide the 'scaffold' for the learning to occur. Vygotsky suggests that there is a *zone of proximal development* (ZPD). This zone is the gap that exists between performance without assistance and performance with assistance. In this model the teacher has a proactive role and has to make the correct analysis of where the pupil is and then provide the appropriate scaffolding. The capacity to learn through instruction and therefore direct teaching is central to these concepts.

Vygotsky's theory of learning finds much support from studies of the functioning of the brain. While we are still not certain how our brains work Abbott (1994) argues that:

> One major discovery, which has revolutionised the way we think about the brain and how it learns, has been the fact that we know that it has plasticity, which means that the physical structure of the brain actually changes as a result of experience. The brain will change if stimulated through interaction with the environment.
>
> (p. 63)

> The brain learns when it is trying to make sense; when it is building on what it already knows, when it recognises the significance of what it is doing; when it is working in complex, multiple perspectives.
>
> (p. 73)

Schools can consciously provide opportunities through curriculum content, teaching styles and the physical and social environment for this stimulation to take place in a challenging but non-threatening way. Providing challenging but non-threatening situations for learners is not easy for schools. For example implementing the national curriculum in a way that recognises and builds on pupils' prior knowledge and skills. If the challenge turns into something the learner perceives as too great and non-attainable the learner is likely to 'drop out'. The optimal state for learning is described by Smith (1996, p. 13) as one of 'relaxed alertness – high challenge and low stress'. The learner will be more likely to meet the challenge if she is able to make connections with previous knowledge. Therein lies the skill of the teacher (a theme we develop in Chapter 3) and his or her ability to make appropriate assessments, and consequently connections, for the learner.

According to Gipps and Murphy (1994, p. 24) learners need to feel a sense of ownership over what they are learning. They need to feel that what they are being taught is relevant to their own purposes. This process has been described as *metacognition:*

> Metacognition is a general term which refers to a second-order form of thinking: thinking about thinking . . . It is a process of being aware of and in control of one's own knowledge and thinking and therefore learning . . . An essential aspect of metacognition is that learners control their own learning and, in order to reflect on the meaning of what they are learning, pupils must feel commitment to it.

There is an interaction therefore between learning, thinking and teaching. The teacher may know what she wants to teach but the learner has control over what is learnt. The teacher may provide the appropriate scaffolding but the learner has to be prepared to use it and motivation to learn is an essential part of the pact between the teacher and learner that we referred to earlier. Teaching the learner the skills of metacognition is likely to be an important motivating factor. This notion finds support in the literature about multiple intelligences. Therefore, as well as being knowledgeable about learning theories, teachers also need to understand the nature of intelligence and that people learn in different ways for different purposes.

Multiple intelligences

Some educationalists question the value of IQ tests as an adequate measure of intelligence, because they only test particular abilities such as verbal and non-verbal reasoning, and do so at one point in time, assuming therefore that intelligence is a fixed entity. David Perkins (1995, p. 115) argues the importance of three distinct dimensions of intelligence: neural, experiential and reflective. He suggests that neural intelligence is, in part, genetically determined but experiential and reflective intelligence can be learned:

> experiential intelligence can be expanded through extensive experience. Reflective intelligence can be expanded through instruction or self-instruction and experience that cultivates metacognition, strategies and attitudes conducive to good thinking.

He goes on to suggest that efforts to cultivate intelligence should focus on reflective intelligence, the control system for neural and experiential intelligence, for example, by providing remembering, problem-solving and decision-making activities:

> Without question two of the three dimensions of intelligence can be advanced by learning – experiential intelligence through in-depth experiences and reflective intelligence through the cultivation of strategies, attitudes and metacognition.

The implication as suggested earlier, is that teachers can provide activities that develop and enhance these aspects of intelligence.

As indicated in Chapter 1, according to the psychologist, Howard Gardner (1983), learners all have the capacity to *develop* at least seven types of intelligence:

1. linguistic: the intelligence of words
2. logical-mathematical: the intelligence of numbers and reasoning
3. spatial: the intelligence of pictures and images
4. musical: the intelligence of tone, rhythm, and timbre

5. bodily-kinaesthetic: the intelligence of the whole body and the hands
6. interpersonal: the intelligence of social understanding
7. intrapersonal: the intelligence of self-knowledge.

Consequently, the question we should be asking of our pupils is not 'how smart are you?' but 'how are you smart?' (MacBeath, 1997, forthcoming).

Gardner's work emphasises that learning is not just about cognition (facts and figures). Daniel Goleman (1996) supports this view. He demonstrates the nature and importance of emotional intelligence and the need to become emotionally literate. This means acknowledging that learning takes place through the senses as well as the mind. It happens by reflecting and analysing on real experience, making connections between new and old experience, making choices and decisions that involve feelings and emotions as well as intellect and reason.

Handy (1997, p. 120) argues that: 'Everyone can be assumed to be intelligent, because intelligence comes in many forms.' From his experience of life he makes his own provisional list of eleven intelligences with the proviso that they need not, and usually do not, correlate with each other:

1. Factual intelligence – the know-it-all facility that Mastermind addicts possess.
2. Analytic intelligence – the ability to reason and to conceptualise.
3. Numerate intelligence – being at ease with numbers of all sorts.
4. Linguistic intelligence – a facility with language and languages.
5. Spatial intelligence – an ability to see patterns in things.
6. Athletic intelligence – the skill exemplified by athletes.
7. Intuitive intelligence – an aptitude for sensing and seeing what is not immediately obvious.
8. Emotional intelligence – self-awareness and self-control, persistence, zeal and self-motivation.
9. Practical intelligence – the ability to recognise what needs to be done and what can be done.
10. Interpersonal intelligence – the ability to get things done with and through others.
11. Musical intelligence – easy to recognise, whether in opera singers, pianists or pop groups.

Handy (1997, p. 120) suggests that:

> A combination of the first three intelligences will get you through most tests and examinations and entitle you to be called clever. But there is more to intelligence than these.

We apply the concept of multiple intelligence to schools in the final chapter. In our definition of *the intelligent school*, we argue that when applying the notion of multiple intelligence to an organisation, as opposed to an individual, successful organisations are those that understand the *interdependent* nature of the different intelligences and strive to develop and use their 'corporate intelligence'.

Howard Gardner and his colleagues (Gardner, 1993a) have developed a programme called Practical Intelligence for Schools (PIFS) which recognises that students need practical coping skills to help with reading, writing and problem-solving as well as more traditional academic skills. PIFS builds on students' understanding of five themes:

knowing why
knowing self
knowing differences
knowing process
reflection.

Each topic taught can be considered in this light.

The PIFS programme also recognises that students have different 'profiles of intelligence' (Gardner, 1993b).

> We might think of the topic as a room with at least five doors or entry points to it. Students vary as to which entry point is most appropriate for them . . . Awareness of these entry points can help the teacher introduce new materials in ways in which they can easily be grasped by a range of students; then, as students explore other entry points, they have the chance to develop those multiple perspectives that are the best antidote to stereotypical thinking.
>
> (Gardner, 1993b, p. 245)

The five entry points suggested are:

- narrational – telling and explaining the story of the topic
- logical-quantitative – using numerical or deductive reasoning processes to understand the concept
- foundational – asking fundamental questions about the topic
- aesthetic – valuing and appreciating sensory experiences
- experiential – having a practical 'hands-on' approach to understanding the concept.

A skilled teacher knows which doors are appropriate for pupils and knows how and when to open them to maximise the potential for learning. MacBeath (1997, forthcoming) argues that it is vital to remember that:

The potential of the brain for learning, is in neurological terms, limitless. It is estimated that there are something like 2,000 billion brain cells each of which has tens of millions of possible connectors, or 'hooks' to other brain cells. In other words there are billions of learning pathways, only a few of which are travelled. The untravelled paths become overgrown and fall into disuse. While this is, in part, a process of ageing, the capacity to learn throughout life, even into old age depends on knowing how to make use of the brain's untapped potential.

Learning styles

Other researchers have identified different learning styles. Dryden and Vos (1994, p. 95, emphasis added), for example, have linked Gardner's work to the way we learn. They believe that each of us has a preferred learning and a preferred working style and identify at least five style preferences:

> Some of us are *mainly* visual learners: we like to see pictures or diagrams. Others are auditory: we like to listen. Others are haptic learners: we learn best by using our sense of touch (tactile learners) or by moving our bodies (kinaesthetic learners). Some are print oriented: we learn easily by reading books. Others are 'group interactive': we learn best when interacting with others.

We can and do use a combination of these strategies to learn but most of us would favour one particular style. Schools may cater well for a few of these styles but not others. No doubt a contributory factor to some pupils becoming disaffected is that they do not have the opportunity to learn in a way that best suits them. By being aware of the range of preferred learning styles and consequently offering a range of teaching styles, we may produce more satisfied customers. Part of this process is selecting the most appropriate style for the type of learning required.

Accelerated learning

Smith (1996, p. 9) describes accelerated learning as:

> an umbrella term for a series of practical approaches to learning which benefit from new knowledge about how the brain functions; motivation and self belief; accessing different sorts of intelligence and retaining and recalling information.

Fundamental to the process which integrates Gardner's seven intelligences described earlier is the expectation that with the right motivation and teaching all learners can reach a level of achievement which previously may have seemed beyond them. Smith's approach (pp. 62–4) is based on knowledge about different learning preferences and a seven-stage accelerated learning cycle. During this cycle the teacher makes connections between previous work and links with the future, explains the content and the outcomes of the lesson (the big picture), uses visual, auditory and kinaesthetic modes (VAK) to put over the content, involves the pupils in appropriate activities designed to understand the content, gives the learner opportunities to demonstrate their understanding of the new knowledge and then allows time for review, for recall and for retention. Joyce *et al.*, (1997) describe a range of strategies teachers can use to accelerate pupils' learning.

What we learn for

Säljö's (1979) interviewing of adults about their understandings of what learning is for identified five different components:

1. Learning as a quantitative increase in knowledge
2. Learning as memorising
3. Learning as the acquisition of facts or procedures which can be used in practical situations
4. Learning as making sense and abstracting meaning
5. Learning as an interpretative process aimed at understanding reality.
(Summarised by Harlen and James, 1996, p. 4)

It would be interesting to ask pupils for their views about what learning is for, although we suspect that their answers would be likely to include the five functions identified by the adults. The important point is that, as Säljö's sample demonstrates, there are different types of learning. Effective and efficient learning must be *learning fit for purpose*.

Researchers, for example Entwistle and Entwistle (1991), have distinguished between *shallow* (sometimes called *surface*) learning and *deep* learning. Shallow learning involves remembering facts without necessarily understanding them. According to Gipps (1994) this can be the type of learning that pupils engage in to prepare for a test or an examination. The likelihood is that the pupils will discard the facts learnt as soon as the need for them has passed. Deep learning, on the other hand, involves understanding the meaning of what is being learnt. Although this type of learning is often described as more desirable than shallow or surface learning, it is important to remember that they both serve a purpose.

> This reminds us that efficient learning is often a combination of both surface and deep learning . . . So if we were to learn everything in depth we would have time to learn very little. Likewise, if everything was surface learning we could hardly describe ourselves as educated at all.
> (Harlen and James, 1996, p. 2).

According to Abbott (1994), there is often a confusion between learning and memory. He suggests that learning is the process by which we acquire new knowledge, and memory is the process by which we retain that knowledge over time. He argues (p. 69) that:

> It is the brain's ability to select what it deems to be of immediate significance, and then act on it in ways that are related to previous experience, that has enabled human beings to rise to a position of mastery over all other species.

In this section we have reflected on some of the theories about learning and highlighted the fact that we learn different things for different reasons and in different ways; so learning, and therefore teaching, has to be fit for purpose. Next, we consider the nature of the learner herself. We pay attention to individual and group differences and then consider the importance of the perception learners have of themselves.

The nature of learners

Learners come in different shapes and sizes

Some children arrive on their first day of school being able to read. Others do not but may have developed an aptitude in other aspects of the curriculum. Some arrive appropriately dressed, well-fed and well-cared for. Some are fit and healthy. Some will enjoy sitting down quietly, speaking and listening to each other and the adults in the classroom. Others will prefer to move around boisterously. Moreover girls and boys may have had different opportunities to develop the different intelligences identified by Gardner. The list of potential differences is very long and does not diminish as people age. The consequence is that all learners will have experienced different learning opportunities and have different learning needs. Some will easily be able to play their part in the learning pact, others will need more encouragement.

Girls and boys: some differences

Several researchers, including Gilligan (1982), Belenky *et al.*, (1986), Tannen (1992) and Gipps and Murphy (1994) have argued that males and females tend to respond differently to the same stimuli or situation. Gilligan, for example, demonstrated how girls tend to consider contexts and analyse the 'whys and wherefores' before making a judgement about a moral dilemma, whereas boys are more likely to create and stick to rules when deciding their opinion. It is important to note that Gilligan does not suggest that girls and boys have different abilities, but that they have different ways of using their abilities: that is, different cognitive styles. (See Figure 2.1.)

Figure 2.1   Helen Cusack in Myers, K. (1992, p. 133).
Reprinted by permission of Helen Cusack.

Calibration, discussed in the previous section, may be very different for males and females as well as for people from different cultures. While there are conflicting theories about why these differences occur there is some evidence that females are more field dependent than males (although there is also criticism of the methodology used in some of the research which demonstrates this). Field dependent learners are interested in the context and relevance of the issue being discussed. Field independent learners are interested in concepts for their own sake.

Murphy (1988, p. 169), for example, argues that:

> Typically girls tend to value the circumstances that activities are presented in and consider that it gives meaning to the issues to be addressed. They do not, therefore, abstract the issues but consider them in relation to the content which then becomes part of the whole problem. Boys as a group, conversely, do consider the issues in isolation judging the context and the content of the activity to be idiosyncratic.

Murphy (1988, p. 170) gives several examples of this phenomenon. One is when primary and secondary age pupils were asked to design a vehicle and a boat to go round the world. As can be seen, the girls and boys in this example had very different perceptions of the same problem:

> The boys' designs were army-type vehicles, sports cars, power boats or battleships. The detail the boys included varied except the majority had elaborate weaponry and next to no living facilities. . . . The girls' boats

were generally cruisers, the vehicles family transport, agricultural machines or children's play vehicles. There was a total absence of weaponry in the girls' designs and a great deal of detail about living quarters and requirements, including food supplies, and cleaning materials (notably absent in the boys' designs).

Head (1996) points out that on occasions a field dependent approach is advantageous and on others a field independent approach is more appropriate. It is not suggested therefore that either way of responding is superior to the other. They are both valuable and sometimes one is preferable in a particular situation. Head (1996, p. 62) argues therefore that:

> Field dependence and independence can be seen as value-free terms. In some contexts, for example locating which component of a car engine is malfunctioning, the extraction mode of thinking is needed. In other contexts, for example in environmental biology, the embedding mode is better, as we would need to consider how a change in one part of the ecosystem affects other parts.

Learners need to develop both ways of responding. Gipps and Murphy (1994) make the point that those who set and mark test papers need to be aware of the different ways in which pupils could respond to the same question.

Some research by Daniels *et al.*, (1996) focuses on special needs in primary classrooms. It demonstrates how much girls help each other to learn and how much more they do this than boys. The researchers speculate that this may have at least three important consequences. First it may help reduce the number of girls needing extra support because they can get it from their peers. Second, the support given is likely to be appropriate because the peers know exactly what type of 'scaffold' is needed. And third, the person giving the support can embed her own learning through the process of teaching someone else. She has extended opportunities to calibrate the information she is passing on.

Boys seem to be more motivated by competition with each other whereas research has found that girls prefer to work in co-operation with each other. Head (1996, p. 64) illustrates this point:

> If two girls are asked to co-operate in painting a picture together they negotiate an agreed plan. Under similar circumstances two boys may simply draw a line down the paper so each has half the page to complete and they then work quite independently.

Cultural differences depending on ethnicity, country of upbringing and class will interplay with gender differences. So, for example, an upper class Asian boy reared in Pakistan is likely to perceive the world differently from a working class Asian boy whose upbringing has been in Tower Hamlets – though they will have race and gender in common. However, Head (1996, pp. 66–7) argues that:

The distribution of gendered roles in the work place shows broad similarities across many cultures. Although there may be regional variations in social practices in detail nevertheless there are enough underlying structural similarities for the explanatory models to have widespread credence. We might therefore expect both gender identities and preferences in cognitive and learning styles to be broadly similar in most cultures.

Head (1996, p. 68) states that the implication of all this for teachers is that if girls and boys

prefer different learning procedures then teachers . . . should be flexible in their choice of teaching and assessment methods. But these gender differences are not absolute, there is considerable overlap between the two sexes and considerable variation within one group. A flexible approach to pedagogy should therefore be of general benefit to the school population.

How learners see themselves

Research evidence demonstrates that social class along with ethnic background, gender and disability appears to exert a considerable influence on life chances. The work of Rosenthal and Jacobson (1968) indicated the impact that teacher expectations have on pupils' learning and therefore their achievement. More recent research has shown how teachers have different expectations of different groups depending on their race, gender and social class. Figure 2.2, for example, shows how teachers predicted higher examination results than were achieved for the English, Scottish and Welsh group but lower for ethnic minority groups.

We have deliberately drawn attention to teachers' expectations in this chapter on learning because of the powerful positive or negative influence such attitudes can have on the type of learning opportunities made available for pupils. In a recent review of the relevant literature, Gillborn and Gipps (1996, p. 58) found that:

A combination of gender and racial stereotypes may make it more difficult for black young men to avoid being caught up in cycles of increasingly severe criticism and control.

Barbara Tizard *et al.*, (1988) examined actions in the home and in the school that appear to affect attainment and progress in the infant school. Particular attention was paid to the different levels of attainment of boys and girls, and of white British children and black British children of Afro-Caribbean origin. The researchers (p. 139) found, as in the 'School Matters' study (Mortimore *et al.*, 1988), that there was a link between disadvantage and pupil progress and attainment. The two most significant school factors that had an impact on outcomes were the taught curriculum and teachers' expectations:

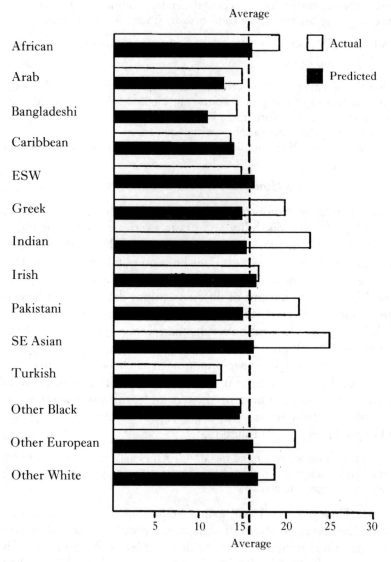

Figure 2.2   Actual and predicted performance scores by ethnic group
Source: Nuttall, 1986.

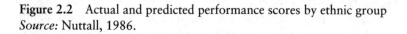

Of the school-based measures we looked at, we found that teachers' academic expectations and children's curriculum coverage showed the strongest and most consistent association with school progress.

When teachers have low expectations of their pupils this can feed into a vicious cycle of underachievement and often poor behaviour. In turn, this can result in many of the pupils underperforming and thus proving the teacher correct. When the opposite happens, particularly with pupils from ethnic minorities and pupils from economically deprived homes who may start off considerably disadvantaged, it helps to build confidence and self-esteem and the all important 'can do' factor. If we believe we can do something, more often than not we are able to do it. We develop the theme of efficacy in Chapter 6.

Other research which has an impact on how the learner sees her or himself includes the suggestion that boys externalise failure, whereas girls are more likely to internalise it and blame themselves (Fennema, 1983). Learning often involves risk-taking. Sometimes this is a private affair between teacher and pupil, for example in an essay. Sometimes it is public, for example when answering questions in class. Learners need to have adequate self-esteem and confidence in order to feel comfortable about taking such risks (Barber, 1993). According to Licht and Dweck (1983), girls and boys receive different feedback from their teachers which has an impact on their self-esteem and may encourage 'learned helplessness' particularly in girls. 'Learned helplessness' is when the learner believes that she or he is helpless and unable to learn.

Learners have different ways of tackling and responding to the same situation. They will make their own sense of the stimuli, depending on their previous experience, their self-esteem and confidence, the social context of the classroom, and the expectations that are held of them. Doing so is their part of the learning pact discussed earlier. Learners also have different expectations of their teachers and of the schools in which they are members and we turn to this issue in the final section.

What learners want

From their teachers

This chapter is concentrating on learning but, as will have become clear to the reader, it is difficult to separate this entirely from teaching (the focus of Chapter 3). We all had teachers that we recall because we remember learning with them. One of us was a head of house, advising year 9 pupils about their option choice and remembers they would frequently want to pursue a subject because they liked the teacher who was teaching them that subject. The school 'line' was that that was not a sensible or mature way to choose subjects to take to examination level. Choices should be made on rational grounds based on future career ambitions rather than emotional and subjective feelings. Although she endorsed the pursuit of 'balance' and widening pupils' aspirations (Myers, 1980) she always harboured feelings that choices based on teachers rather than subject content were actually just as sensible and rational.

As adult learners, the three of us know that we learn better whatever the topic, if we find the teacher at the very least empathetic, interesting and ideally inspiring. We like the teacher to explain the topic well, not to make us feel stupid when we do not understand immediately, and to treat us as someone who may have something interesting to say on the topic. We like to be stretched and challenged but also to be allowed to challenge conventional wisdom. We suspect that we are not alone here and that these preferences are common to all ages and stages of learning.

Over the last two years, one of us has informally interviewed young people in a number of schools about their views on their education. Their answers to questions about how they learn are almost always the same, whatever their age. They say they learn best with teachers who:

- explain things well
- listen to them and are concerned about them as an individual
- show them how to get better
- keep control of the class
- have a sense of humour.

In response to a question in a survey asking pupils in one secondary school to describe a good teacher the following were typical responses A good teacher is someone:

- who helps you do your work
- who can control the class
- who listens to me
- you can talk to and ask them when you are worried or stuck
- who helps you and teaches you something
- who is good with kids, can control kids, who knows what they are doing
- who has a laugh but gets some hard work done.

A year 10 pupil summed up the general feeling:

> A good teacher is someone who, if you don't understand the work, explains it to you patiently. Isn't too strict but when pupils are being pathetic, can control them, and you can talk to and have a laugh with him/her.
>
> (Myers, 1996a)

Jean Rudduck and colleagues (Rudduck, Chaplain and Wallace, 1996, p. 1) have emphasised the importance of asking the learner about her/his needs. In their study called Making Your Way Through Secondary School, they tracked pupils during their last four years of secondary schooling. They claim that although the pupils were very appreciative of the support and time they received from their teachers, they felt that the *conditions of learning* they were subjected to did not adequately take account of their social maturity:

> nor of the tensions and pressures they feel as they struggle to reconcile the demands of their social and personal lives with the development of their identity as learners.

The authors consequently suggest six principles that would make a significant difference to learning. They acknowledge that the conditions are not new and that many schools will have already incorporated them in their practice. However, the importance of these principles outlined below is that they are presented from the pupils' perspective; not what we think is good for them, but what they think is good for themselves.

1. Respect for pupils as individuals and as a body occupying a significant position in the institution of the school.
2. Fairness to all pupils irrespective of their class, gender, ethnicity or academic status.
3. Autonomy – not as an absolute state but as both a right and a responsibility in relation to physical and social maturity.
4. Intellectual challenge that helps pupils to experience learning as a dynamic, engaging and empowering activity.
5. Social support in relation to both academic and emotional concerns.
6. Security in relation to both the physical setting of the school and in interpersonal encounters (including anxiety about threats to pupils' self-esteem).

(Ruddock, Chaplain and Wallace, 1996, p. 174)

To create appropriate conditions of learning, the authors suggest that we need to consider organisational structures and pupil–teacher relationships. They also argue (p. 174) that in addition:

> pupils need to have a sense of themselves as a learner; status in the school; an overall purpose in learning; control over their own lives; and a sense of their future.

From the environment – physical, emotional and social

Appropriate, attractive and well-cared-for physical conditions are not a substitute for good teaching but they can support and facilitate learning. An attractive, welcoming, comfortable and safe environment, with access to adequate appropriate resources, enables learning to take place and we refer to this again in Chapter 3. Schools that take these requirements seriously will take account of individual circumstances by, for example, considering: what is 'safe' for pupils who are racially harassed on their way to and from school; how people whose first language is not English may be encouraged to feel welcome; how pupils who do not have access to the latest technology at home can have this opportunity during and outside school hours. We can learn in different conditions (and in some parts of the world students have to), but it is much easier to do so when conditions help, rather than hinder, learning.

External physical conditions can aid learning but learners also have internal requirements. For example, we are likely to be more responsive to learning if we are not hungry and not cold. Some learners are 'morning people' and some prefer to work late at night (the latter being difficult to cater for in schools that are open 9.00–4.00). In addition, we have emotional and social needs and preferences.

> Emotion plays a vital part in learning. It is in many ways the key to the brain's memory system. And the emotional content of any presentation can play a big part in how readily learners absorb information and ideas.
> (Dryden and Vos, 1994, p. 351)

Some learners respond well to a competitive classroom environment, others do not. Some learners prefer to learn on their own and others learn best by working with other people. This preference may have as much to do with the task in hand as with the favoured learning need. Some learners prefer to work in peace and quiet, others like background noise such as music and others like to work in the midst of hustle and bustle. One of our colleagues who has her own office chooses to write her academic papers in the midst of the comings and goings of the secretaries' office. When questioned about this she explains that she cannot work in silence.

Schools may find it difficult to respond to these varied preferences but during the course of the day or the week it should be possible to ensure that learners experience a range of conditions, some of which will suit them more than others.

Conclusion

In this chapter we have reflected on theories about learning, stressed that learners have different learning needs and preferred styles and discussed what learners say they want from their teachers and schools. We have suggested that learning involves a pact. This pact is between the learner and whoever (for example, a teacher, a friend) or whatever (for example, a computer, a book) the learner is interacting with. The learner must want to learn and must give consent to learn.

The job of the school is: to motivate the learner; to encourage her or him to want to learn; to help the learner understand how to learn; and to *believe that it is possible* to do so. The learner controls whatever he or she is learning through the processes of calibration and metacognition. In this way, the learner makes her own sense of what is being taught. This will be dependent on many factors such as the learner's prior experiences, her self-esteem, her heritage, her attitude to learning and her attitude to what is being taught. It will also be dependent *on the way* she is being taught. This part of the process is usually in the control of the teacher. As well as being knowledgeable about what she is teaching, the teacher's side of the pact is to be aware of these factors, in order to be able to assess what is needed and to provide the appropriate 'scaffolding' and conditions for that particular learner to move on. Learning can take place when both parties are willing and able to fulfil their side of the pact. The following chapter looks at the implications of all of this for teaching.

Questions for discussion

1. Think of something you have learnt recently. Track back the process involved. Does it match with the section on theories about learning?

2. What are the implications of the section on theories about learning for your classroom practice?

3. What is your preferred learning style? Visual, auditory, haptic or another? How does this influence your teaching style?

4. Do the girls in your classes support each other in different ways from the boys? If so, does this matter? Can you/should you do anything about it?

5. Ask your pupils how they prefer to learn. Do their answers surprise you? Do they differ depending on their age or ability (or some other variable such as sex) or is there considerable consensus? Are your teaching styles appropriate for your pupils' learning needs?

6. Do you agree that learning is a pact between the teacher and learner? How can you motivate pupils to want to learn with you?

3

Learning about effective teaching

Effective teachers are those that provide pupils with maximum opportunity to learn.

(Silcock, 1993, p. 13).

The previous chapter considered the nature of learning, learners and
what learners want. This chapter explores the nature of teaching and
related issues. It focuses on what we need to know about the main
characteristics of effective teaching in the light of what we have discovered about effective learning. We discuss what it is that *intelligent
schools* can do to support the development of teaching that will promote
effective learning.

There are many interesting aspects to effective teaching often connected with teachers' own histories and biographies (Fullan and
Hargreaves, 1994). We also know that the particular context in which
teachers find themselves influences the effectiveness of their practice. For
example, studies have shown that the range of practices between classrooms within the same school, can be greater than the differences between schools (Mortimore *et al.,* 1988). For the purposes of this book,
however, we focus on the craft of the classroom and what it is that
teachers do there to enable learning to be enhanced and effective. The
chapter identifies the characteristics of effective teaching to help readers
consider and reflect on them and their relationship with each other.

We begin by addressing the question – what is the purpose of teaching? – and continue with a consideration of the knowledge, skills and
understanding needed for effective teaching.

The purpose of teaching

Effective teaching needs to be considered in the context of the *purpose* of
teaching. Discussions about teaching are very topical, with great attention being paid to popularised and polarised views about what constitutes 'good' and 'bad' teaching. This discussion is often characterised
more by opinion than by close attention to what we actually know about

effective teaching. Much of the discussion also tends to focus on the *style* of the teaching rather than its purpose. In our view, *teaching is the responsibility that schools have for ensuring that pupils are learning about their world, each other and themselves.* This point was well made by the educational philosopher Paul Hirst (1974, p. 105) over twenty years ago: 'The intention of all teaching activities is that of bringing about learning.' He goes on to say that this is a simple but crucial idea: 'It involves the claim that the concept of teaching is in fact totally unintelligible without a grasp of the concept of learning.'

A school's primary task is the structuring and organising of learning, together with the responsibility for the standard and quality of the learning *outcomes* achieved by the pupils. Not surprisingly, the relationship between effective teaching and pupil outcomes has become the focus of considerable attention in recent years.

Effective teaching is comprised of a set of interrelated skills, knowledge and understandings in the mind of the teacher that interact with skills, knowledge and understandings in the minds of pupils, to enable effective learning and high achievement to occur. Teaching and learning are like a good relationship; they have their separate and different identities but depend for their success and well-being on the way they relate to each other and work together.

The debate about how a teacher should teach is not a straightforward one, particularly in the light of new understandings about human growth and development. Our developing understandings about learning, and an awareness of the importance of pupils' perceptions about their own learning, mean that discussions about teaching need to be handled carefully, and from a sound evidence base. There is no single, simple way to teach because there is no single way to learn and there is no doubt that the teacher's task is becoming increasingly complex and sophisticated. This became clear in the reflections on learning theories and learning styles discussed in the previous chapter.

The characteristics of effective teaching

In our discussion we draw from four sources of evidence about the characteristics of effective teaching. They are:

- the experience of teachers based on their classroom practice

- research into effective teaching

- observations of teaching, inspection, training student teachers, teacher appraisal and

- what the pupils have to say themselves.

From these sources we suggest there are three core aspects that together constitute effective teaching:

- knowledge and understanding about the content of teaching

- knowledge and understanding about how pupils learn

- knowledge and understanding about how to manage the process of learning and teaching.

Each involves knowledge, understanding and skill on the part of the teacher and each is dependent for its success on the other two. We now consider these in turn.

Knowledge and understanding about the content of teaching

Subject knowledge

The minimum requirement for this aspect in the 1990s is that teachers have an understanding and knowledge about the national curriculum. Effective teaching, however, requires a good deal more than simply that. Primary teachers need a thorough grasp of subjects across the key stages if progression and continuity are to be handled appropriately. Secondary teachers need to know where their subject fits into or alongside other subject areas. For example, a mathematics department needs to know how the geographers are teaching data handling and statistics, and an art department should know how the historians deal with painters in the period being studied. Secondary teachers can also draw on and make connections with the content of lessons that pupils are studying both before and after their own lessons.

As well as requiring subject knowledge in the appropriate key stage, primary teachers need to have a realistic sense of how the subjects fit together in order to achieve balance and avoid overload. Effective curriculum planning is an essential component of effective teaching.

Over thirty years ago J. S. Bruner (1960, p. 31) argued for a focus on what he then termed 'fundamentals':

> The curriculum of a subject should be determined by the most fundamental understanding that can be achieved of the underlying principles that give structure to that subject.

An article by Preston Feden (1994, p. 20, emphasis added) agrees with this.

> Because truly useful understanding takes time to develop, it is usually not possible for teachers to cover as much curriculum, or as many topics, as they typically attempt . . . the point is to lead pupils to a deep understanding of what is covered. Lessons and units of study designed around *core*

concepts are more likely to produce conceptual change that moves learners along from novice to expert in subject matter content. Teaching for understanding is a crucial responsibility of the job and therefore being able to relate to subject matter in ways that enable genuine understanding is a central task for teachers.

One challenge, as discussed in Chapter 2, is to achieve the right kind of balance between shallow and deep learning. Another challenge is to ensure balance across the curriculum. Schools can now use the national curriculum programmes of study to provide them with the key skills and concepts that need to be taught. Effective teaching, however, is characterised by the teacher's ability to construct learning experiences in a way that builds on pupils' prior knowledge both in particular subjects, and across the curriculum. It is our observation that even more could be done to organise subject planning around key themes, skills and concepts and that this could reduce the sense of overload that the national curriculum can give and encourage greater understanding for pupils as well as enable them to relate more systematically to their prior learning.

Knowledge of learning skills

Essential to most effective teaching is the need for teachers to know how to help their pupils acquire and develop learning skills. These include how to find out, conduct research or enquire into the subject matter in hand. An important learning skill that relates centrally to the content of teaching is the ability pupils need to carry out a process of enquiry. This applies across the school age range. Pupils not only need to know where to find appropriate information but how to extract, interpret and make sense and use of it. This involves bringing together the teaching of research skills and information handling across the curriculum and across the key stages so that higher order reading skills, the skill of writing information in the pupil's own words, structuring arguments and asking deeper questions are then all used in the service of the process of enquiry. This is at the heart of academic study. It is vital that these skills are taught, practised, honed and sharpened throughout a pupil's school life.

Sometimes subject-focused enquiry has been seen as an alternative to instruction by the teacher, rather than the planned practice and experience the pupils need in studying and applying the fruits of instruction. Rigour has often been lacking in the structuring and teaching of the enquiry process, and consequently the debates about teaching have been rightly critical of classroom activity that has been undemanding and, at times, merely successful in keeping pupils occupied. It is our view that teaching could often be more effective if greater attention was paid to the teaching of the skills needed for subject study including how to use tools, materials and equipment effectively. Effective teaching reflects the key principles of the subject as well as particular skills pupils need to learn about subjects effectively.

Knowledge and understanding about how pupils learn

As we discussed in Chapter 2, teachers need to know and understand how pupils learn. In this chapter we discuss how effective teaching reflects our understanding about effective learning. We have asserted that the learning process will vary depending on what is to be learnt and by whom. It will also vary depending on the ages of the pupils and their particular stages of development. Learning activities and lessons need to be designed to reflect this understanding. Howard Gardner (1993b, p. 253) writes that 'we must place ourselves inside the heads of our students and try to understand as far as possible the sources and strengths of their conceptions'.

At one time it seemed to be sufficient to define ourselves as a 'traditional teacher' or 'child-centred' or 'whole-class teacher' or 'more comfortable working with groups'. However, experience and research about teaching, together with what we now know about learning, mean that the *learning to be undertaken* rather than our personal preferences as teachers needs to underpin choices about our teaching styles. According to Bruner (1996, p. 48):

> Once we recognize that a teacher's conception of a learner shapes the instruction he or she employs, then equipping teachers (or parents) with the best available theory of the child's mind becomes crucial.

As we argued in Chapter 2, learning and therefore teaching has to be fit for the purpose in hand. This has implications that are exciting as well as challenging because there is always something new to discover about how to develop and organise effective learning; teachers do not have to confine themselves to a particular style. We know that both the learners and the learning require different things from us at different times. Effective teaching is characterised by a broad range of teaching styles that reflect the learning in progress and the purpose of the teaching. It is also characterised by a willingness to develop new strategies and improve existing ones.

The design of learning

Knowledge about learners and learning as described in Chapter 2 needs to be applied to the careful *design of learning* by the teacher. The challenge, as Schulman (1987) suggests, is that effective teaching requires our subject knowledge to be translated into teaching programmes that meet the learning needs of our pupils. We know from our knowledge

Table 3.1 Summary of the 'seven ways of teaching'

Intelligence	Teaching activities (examples)	Teaching materials (examples)	Instructional strategies
Linguistic	lectures, discussions, word games, storytelling, choral reading, journal writing, etc.	books, tape recorders, typewriters, stamp sets, books on tape, etc.	read about it, write about it, talk about it, listen to it.
Logical-Mathematical	brain teasers, problem-solving, science experiments, mental calculation, number games, critical thinking, etc.	calculators, maths manipulatives, science equipment, maths games, etc.	quantify it, think critically about it, conceptualise it.
Spatial	visual presentations, art activities, imagination games, mind-mapping, metaphor, visualisation, etc.	graphs, maps, video, LEGO sets, art materials, optical illusions, cameras, picture library, etc.	see it, draw it, visualise it, color it, mind-map it.
Bodily-Kinaesthetic	hands-on learning, drama, dance, sports that teach, tactile activities, relaxation exercises, etc.	building tools, clay, sports equipment, manipulatives, tactile learning resources, etc.	build it, act it out, touch it, get a 'gut feeling' of it, dance it.
Musical	superlearning, rapping, songs that teach.	tape recorder, tape collection, musical instruments	sing it, rap it, listen to it.
Interpersonal	co-operative learning, peer tutoring, community involvement, social gatherings, simulations, etc.	board games, party supplies, props for role plays, etc.	teach it, collaborate on it, interact with respect to it.
Intrapersonal	individualised instruction, independent study, options in course of study, self-esteem building, etc.	self-checking materials, journals, materials for projects, etc.	connect it to your personal life, make choices with regard to it.

Source: Armstrong, 1994, p. 52.

about learning that subject expertise is not enough in itself. Teachers also have to be skilled in designing learning experiences, activities and opportunities for the pupils. As we discussed in Chapter 2, children have the capacity to develop at least seven intelligences (Gardner, 1983). Armstrong (1994) has taken this list of intelligences and suggested possible teaching activities linked to them. This practical application of Gardner's intelligences is illustrated in Table 3.1.

There are four main design components to maximise effective classroom learning. It must:

- have clear intentions
- be well structured
- be well organised
- be well matched to the pupils' previous learning and appropriate to their stage of development.

We look at these in turn.

Clear intentions

Demonstrating the importance of *learning intentions* linked to the design of the teaching process is crucial. Learning intentions, if they are clear and accurate, are like route planners for a journey. We need to know something about the direction we are going in, the kind of terrain we are likely to cover and how long it might take, in order to make decisions about the equipment we need, prior skills and knowledge necessary and the best way to get there. We do not know whether we have arrived even approximately near to our destination without them.

When it comes to learning there are so many possible skills, knowledge, understandings (and any combinations of all three) that could be utilised, that successful learning requires both the teacher and pupils to be quite clear what the particular intentions are for a lesson or series of activities. These intentions need to be drawn from different aspects of the learning in progress: social and cross-curricular as well as related to the subject.

The discussion about learning intentions has sometimes tended to be confused with discussions about attainment. Here the term 'learning intentions' is used rather than 'learning outcomes' because it is not realistic to assume to know precise outcomes for pupils for each individual lesson and there have been many critiques of behavioural objectives in the educational literature, for example, Eisner (1985). However, we do have a responsibility to know what the learning outcomes are as they emerge and to use this information to monitor the appropriateness of what is being learnt for both individual pupils and the class as a whole. We return to this aspect of effective teaching later in the chapter.

Structuring for learning

Observations of teaching suggest the *structure* of a lesson, activity or series of these needs also to be designed carefully. Structure is achieved through a range of different processes in the classroom that support learning. Some of these processes are derived from the subject material; for example, the teaching of a chronological series of events, the different stages in a science experiment, the cooking of a cake. Others relate more to the process of teaching and learning which we consider in the next section. Structure is predominantly the way in which the learning experience is put together in advance so that it can be a coherent, interesting, accessible and progressive experience for the particular pupils involved. This is where the skill of knowing which door to open (see p. 25, Chapter 2) is important.

This is also where the issue about whole-class teaching, group or individual work is brought into debate. We believe that effective sessions in classrooms are usually a healthy mixture of the three. A recent literature review of classroom conditions for school improvement (Beresford, 1995) reinforces this point and identifies, as we have already done, a wide teaching repertoire as an essential classroom condition. What is important is that there is a structured approach with clear reasons for the choice of structure, matched to the learning intentions for a particular lesson. Similarly there needs to be a structure for a session or series of lessons, that has a clear introduction, middle and conclusion. This will include explanations and instruction from the teacher, and experience by the pupils of the process of drawing together what has happened, reflecting on it and planning next steps. Criticisms of teaching are often related to the absence of a sufficient structure within the design of the learning for the pupils and hence in the lesson or activity itself.

Organising for learning

A well-organised classroom supports learning and encourages the pupils to become well-organised themselves. Our experience suggests that this aspect of effective teaching has been a little neglected whilst the national curriculum demands have been put in place. In several of the projects that we have been involved with recently on learning and teaching, participants have returned to the centrality of the quality of the classroom environment as a basis for effectiveness. Indeed, most of the national curriculum cannot be satisfactorily delivered if resources are not to hand and the pupils are not being taught the skills of how to use them.

Matching the learning to the learners

The fourth aspect of learning design is probably the most complex for the majority of teachers. It is the process of erecting the appropriate scaffolding, as discussed in the previous chapter, to enable learning to take place. The teacher has a responsibility to *match* the pupils' previous learning and abilities to the current teaching context in order to ensure progress. This is often interpreted as an issue about individualising planning, which can seem very daunting given the size of classes and the range of needs that teachers are often facing. It needs to be interpreted, instead, as an issue about the use of a range of design skills to achieve the best fit between the learners and what is to be learnt.

If an effective teacher is one who gives pupils maximum opportunity to learn, then it is important to know how to design learning so that all pupils are able, as far as possible, to gain access to it and also to make progress. The research literature suggests that the appropriate match of the pupils to the learning experience has a significant impact on their achievement (Bennett *et al.*, 1984; Galton, 1980, 1989). The challenge is to find ways to manage the pupils' access to learning whilst maintaining the momentum of the curriculum content to be covered. Attention needs to be paid to both. A recent review (Tabberer, 1996, p. 5) highlighted the importance of appropriate challenge in teaching:

> Research studies have added to the evidence that teachers too rarely provide children with tasks which are genuinely demanding and open ended. Teachers have been observed spending on average only 2 per cent of classroom time on questions regarded as offering challenge.

There seem to be at least four kinds of design skills that effective teachers use that help them to match and differentiate within their overall class plan. First, they are always adding to a sound knowledge base about their pupils' learning strengths, weaknesses and preferences as outlined in Chapter 2. Formative assessment, in the sense of gathering information about learning whilst it is in progress, is seen by effective teachers as part of good teaching, and ways of collecting it that are straightforward and realistic are part of the culture of the classroom. Some assessments are recorded and deliberate and some are unprompted and not written down. Some involve the pupils quite fully and some the teacher keeps to herself. This means that classroom life is organised in a way that enables the teacher not just to *support* pupils' learning but also to give feedback on their performance. The teacher can then *diagnose* learning responses and needs, and note the progress that is being made. This is the 'feedforward' function of assessment and its presence in practice greatly contributes to effective teaching.

The importance of using assessment information in planning cannot be underestimated. Our view is that monitoring and diagnosis, planned as part of teaching and not viewed as something separate, should play a greater part in learning design and its implementation. Time needs to be allocated on a regular basis as part of the planning process for the teacher to gather information about the learning in progress in the class. This might be a running reading record with an individual pupil, particular questions to ask a group at work on a science task or a simple test to the whole class on a humanities topic. Methods will vary, the point is to know what information is needed and how it builds a picture of the whole class over time as well as noting any significant individual learning problems that might also need wider referral. Most important of all is the use that the teacher makes of the information gathered to inform the planning of teaching. We can begin to see that what distinguishes effective teaching here is that it gives priority to gathering as well as imparting information. This theme is developed further in Chapter 5.

Second, effective teachers are very skilled in the way that they plan to group their pupils and think through how they are going to spend their time to meet the needs of different groups. Whilst the pupils in a primary class may have a 'base group' to which they belong, they may well come together in different combinations for different activities based on their identified learning needs. Pupil grouping in this sort of classroom is a quite deliberate part of the learning design. It is flexible, with the primary purpose of enabling learning to take place. The teacher has a clear notion, planned in advance, about the nature of the intervention and support teaching that she is going to provide. This reinforces again the importance of balancing whole-class teaching with group activities, both to support the pupils' learning and also to consolidate the teacher's knowledge about the curriculum as it is being received by the pupils.

Third, effective teachers design into their learning plan particular opportunities for pupils to practise and rehearse skills and knowledge in which they are needing further work. This is not a learning programme for every child, but it is a known time when pupils in consultation with their teacher can make progress by having the time to consolidate or gain more experience in a piece of learning. Support staff and parents can also be involved in this process.

Finally, when matching the learning to the learners, effective teachers build into the learning design quality extension activities for pupils to engage in if they finish a task before others in the class. 'Fast finishers' in a primary classroom can move to a reading game or a design they are preparing or a letter that needs completing, whilst secondary age pupils can do some further extension or consolidation work in the subject concerned. Match is not just giving pupils work that is pitched to a level they can meet and then extending learning by giving them more of the same activity. It needs also to stretch and challenge pupils and give colour and variety to learning.

Having considered the knowledge, skills and understanding that a teacher needs to have about both subjects and the design of the learning process, we now bring these together into delivery in the classroom and the actual experience of managing the teaching and learning process as it is happening. This is our third core aspect of effective teaching.

Managing the process of teaching and learning

This is the heart of effective teaching, where the teaching and the learning are in dynamic interaction. Effective teachers know that this is the main activity in which they are engaged.

In his search for indicators of effective teaching, Schulman (1987) observed several teachers in a research programme over three years and he comments on how both content knowledge and pedagogical strategies necessarily interact in the minds of teachers and in their classroom practice. This answers the old question asked of one of us quite recently, 'do we teach subjects or children?' Our reflections on effective teaching suggest unequivocally that we must do both.

In our view there are two main features of the 'live' teaching and learning process that contribute to its effectiveness. These are:

● a style that emphasises instruction as well as reflection

● respect for the learners and their learning process.

The first pays attention in action to the subject of the lesson and the second to the learners and the learning. We have already noted that an effective teaching style is not just about the way the pupils are organised. It is also about the way learning is enabled to take place. Effective teaching in action is in essence good communication. It is a complex and sophisticated craft when it is done well, because in a good classroom there are different types of communication going on at the same time. There is instructional communication linked to the subject matter and the learning process, and interactive communication linked to the relationship with the learners.

Much of the research literature refers to the importance of instructional strategies as a characteristic of effective teaching. These it would seem are most effective when sufficient emphasis is given to *direct* as well as *indirect* instruction; the first when the teacher is directly teaching pupils and the second when the pupils are working on a task or activity. The 'Three Wise Men' report (Alexander, Rose and Woodhead, 1992), for example, suggested that indirect teaching has been promoted at the expense of direct teaching. A particular example given was an overemphasis on work sheets and scheme books that were not sufficiently linked for the pupils to any practical context or explicit skills development.

Schulman (1987, pp. 13–14) suggests that instructional teaching in most subject matter needs to emphasise four distinct components particularly for intellectual development: comprehension, reasoning, transformation and reflection:

> The image of teaching involves the exchange of ideas. The idea is grasped, probed, and comprehended by the teacher, who then must turn it about in his or her mind, seeing many sides of it. Then the idea is shaped or tailored until it can in turn be grasped by students. This grasping, however, is not a passive act. Just as the teacher's comprehension requires a vigorous interaction with the ideas, so students will be expected to encounter ideas actively as well. Indeed our exemplary teachers present ideas in order to provoke the constructive processes of their students and not to incur student dependence on teachers or to stimulate the flatteries of imitation.

It is here that the process of enquiry described earlier in the chapter comes into play as part of effective teaching. Comprehension is not enough. Teachers have also to be able to transform their pupils' understandings so that the skills of analysis, hypothesis, judgement and then application can be developed. For, as Bruner (1960, p. 17) asserted in his earliest writings:

> The first object of any act of learning . . . is that it should serve us in the future. Learning should not only take us somewhere, it should allow us to go further more easily.

What seems to be coming through from these sources is that what is defined as instructional teaching is not observed, as traditionally thought, to be the sole domain of the teacher. Quite the contrary. Effective teaching enables what Schulman (1987) describes as the constructive processes of the pupils: it engages them *actively* in learning. This is another function of scaffolding referred to in Chapter 2.

This is echoed in the findings of the ORACLE study by Galton and colleagues (Galton, 1980) and in subsequent studies (Galton, 1989). In her review of Galton's work, Gipps (1992, p. 13) comments that:

> What comes through again and again from Galton's work is the importance of *high levels of questioning* and the need to engage in strategies which allow *maximum levels of sustained interaction* with all pupils.

The fourth instructional strategy Schulman refers to is reflection. Effective teaching pays attention to checking what has been covered with the pupils, examining and articulating what has been learnt, encouraging them to present their thoughts, findings and opinions. The teacher has an important role in summarising what has happened and encouraging the pupils to do the same. This provides the pupils with the additional skills of being able to talk about learning which supports their engagement with it and deepens their comprehension and mastery. It supports, therefore, the process of calibration described in Chapter 2.

There are a second set of strategies that effective teachers use which reflect their understanding of both the learning process and the learners themselves. These are oriented to the relationship the teacher has with the pupils, the pupils' engagement with their learning, the respect and the expectations the teacher has for them and the support she offers to them. *The intelligent school* understands the importance of the combined use of these strategies; a theme we develop in the final chapter.

Research undertaken almost twenty years ago (Soar and Soar, 1979) showed that both neutral and warm emotional climates have a strong correlation with achievement, whereas a negative atmosphere can be dysfunctional and is likely to affect the pupils' progress. This suggests that the quality of the relationships the teacher has with her class is not just desirable in itself but has an impact on the quality of the learning. A study by Good and Brophy (1986) found that pupils did not achieve as well if their teacher was attending to her relationship with them at the expense of instructional teaching. This reinforces our earlier view that effective teaching pays attention to both the learners and to what is being taught.

A beginning teacher evaluation study (Powell, 1980, p. 9) found that more effective teachers 'call their students by name, attend carefully to what they say, accept their statements of feeling, praise their successes and involve them in decision making.' This accords with the finding in the school effectiveness literature that the acknowledgement of pupil rights and responsibilities is a characteristic of effective schools (see Chapter 1, p. 6)

The humanistic psychologist Carl Rogers (1982) cites some research undertaken in the 1970s by Aspy and Roebuck (1976) which examined teacher behaviour in relation to learning outcomes for the pupils. They found three things that characterised a clear correlation between the facilitative conditions provided by the teacher and the academic achievement of the pupils:

- The teachers displayed their humanness to their pupils and were committed to the pupils' success.

- There was a high level of respect, interest in and acceptance of the pupils.

- The teachers demonstrated an empathy towards the pupils that showed that they cared about the quality of life for them in the classroom.

The pupils, as a result, were more academically successful, had a more positive self-concept, exhibited fewer discipline problems and had a lower absence rate from school. This kind of classroom climate is endorsed by the pupils' views described in Chapter 2 along with the impact of teachers' expectations also referred to in that chapter.

Our own observations and experience suggest that the pupils' participation in their learning is also central to their success. This is not just in terms of interactive instruction and planned intervention to support learning, important though this is. Our work suggests that achievement is enhanced when pupils are enabled to understand what they are doing and why they are doing it. This relates to issues raised about metacognition in Chapter 2, and is an important aspect of what is implied by 'purposeful teaching', another key characteristic identified in the effective schools literature.

Returning to Bruner (1996), pupils need to understand the intentions for learning that are in the mind of the teacher. In addition, pupils need to be taught the skills of identifying their mistakes and using strategies to improve their work so that they too can have a role in classroom assessment. As far as possible they need to be involved not just in recognising their achievement, but also in diagnosing what they need to do next to improve. That is why the greater emphasis on positive feedback to pupils about their learning through processes like the 'Records of Achievement' initiative has been so important. The way work is marked is also an opportunity for pupils to gain important insights into both their success and strategies for improvement. Our observations suggest that this process can begin at a young age.

Conclusion: the Teaching and Learning PACT

This chapter has examined our own experience and that of other practitioners, together with some of the research findings about what constitutes effective teaching. We have argued that teaching is a complex and sophisticated craft when it is done well. It is composed of distinct but interrelated parts and cannot be separated from its relationship to learning.

In Chapter 2 we suggested that effective learning involves a *pact* between the learner and the teacher. Figure 3.1 summarises Chapters 2 and 3 by drawing together the key features of this pact to illustrate what it looks like in action in the classroom. The Figure shows what the learner and the teacher bring to the learning and teaching situation and, in turn, what they both need to bring to enable the pact to have maximum effect.

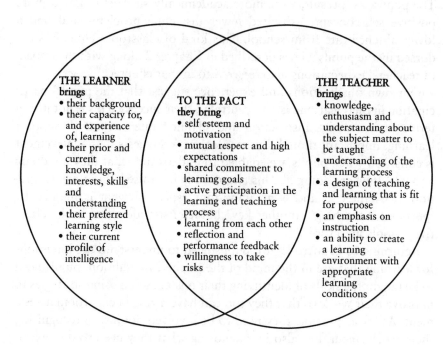

Figure 3.1   The teaching and learning PACT – the interdependence of the teacher and learner
© 1997 B. MacGilchrist, K. Myers and J. Reed

Questions for discussion

1. Do you agree with the characteristics of effective teaching identified in this chapter? Would you add to them?

2. What guidance is available in your school that supports the promotion of effective teaching? How can it be improved?

3. Which of the research findings about teaching identified in the chapter do you think would be most helpful to discuss at your school?

4. To what extent has your school identified principles that would support the design of learning activities for the pupils?

4

Teachers' learning

If you are travelling with small children on an aeroplane, the flight attendant tells you in the case of emergency to put the oxygen mask on yourself first in order that you are in a position to help your child.

(Roland Barth, 1990, p. 46)

In the previous two chapters we reflected on learning and examined the characteristics of effective teaching. We suggested that learning is a life-long activity. We discussed the complexity and challenges of teaching competently given the current climate of high expectations and the multifarious demands placed on teachers. In this chapter we again take up the theme of learning and now focus on teachers' learning. We discuss why teachers need to learn; how they can learn 'on the job'; the opportunities that exist for learning outside school; and ways to encourage teachers' learning. We draw on examples from schools that illustrate how teachers can learn through working together to improve teaching and learning for pupils. In conclusion, we suggest that teachers' learning and pupils' learning are inextricably linked.

Why do teachers need to learn?

Teachers need to keep up to date with their area of expertise and with recent research about pedagogy. They have to keep up to date with legislative changes that affect their work such as the national curriculum, assessment, inspection and appraisal. Learning needs to be continuous in order to enable teachers to improve classroom practice, contribute to whole-school issues, take on new roles and responsibilities, manage change and acquire new skills. Barth (1990, p. 49) suggests that

nothing within a school has more impact on students in terms of skills' development, self confidence or classroom behaviour than the personal and professional development of teachers.

Likewise, Joyce and Showers (1988) argue that learning for teachers can have a significant impact on pupil achievement.

In the near future it is likely that teachers will have to gain qualifications overseen by the Teacher Training Agency (TTA) in order to obtain promotion. But learning in *the intelligent school* is more than keeping up to date because you have to, or obtaining qualifications because you must. Learning in this school is about a continual quest to do the job even better. It involves acknowledging, as we said in Chapter 3, that effective teaching is not a fixed set of skills and knowledge but is constantly evolving and adapting to the needs of different groups of pupils. It is a continuous process not an event. Support for teachers' own learning and development is a key characteristic of *the intelligent school*. This applies to individuals, to groups of teachers in year or department teams, and to the whole school as an institution. In this context, the needs of individuals as well as the institution have to be acknowledged. Individual teachers need to be involved with whole-school learning initiatives. They must also have the opportunity to fulfil their own personal, professional needs.

There are many advantages if the funding for inservice activities is delegated to individual schools. Schools can agree their needs and plan to meet them in a coherent manner. The one main disadvantage is that this way of funding does not encourage a long-term view of inservice education. Why should schools pay for the inservice needs of an individual who may move on to another institution that will reap the benefit of this process? With limited resources, how do you balance individual needs with those of the institution? We believe that staff development has to be seen as an investment in the future. We also believe that teachers who enjoy learning opportunities are more likely to enjoy their job, more likely to enthuse others (colleagues and pupils) and more likely to remain in the profession. *The intelligent school* is prepared to make this investment because it understands the significance of contributing to a climate that values the importance of continual learning. This sense of moral purpose is developed in Chapter 6.

Addington, a special school in Reading, deals with this issue by allocating every teacher and teacher assistant eight days every year for their professional development. One-third of this time is for their subject responsibility. The next third is for school self-evaluation. This is used by choosing a topic from the school development plan that is due to be evaluated. Two teachers, one classroom assistant and the quality assurance manager discuss how this could and should be evaluated, carry out the process during a term and then report their findings to the rest of the staff. Being involved in such an activity that offers opportunities for collaboration, discussion and presentation becomes a professional development experience and also fulfils a valuable function for the school. The remaining time is for the staff's own personal professional development and this is personally negotiated with their line-manager. Teachers in this school maintain their own personal development portfolios (described by the head as a running record of achievement for teachers) in order to plan and take charge of their own professional development.

How can teachers learn?

Learning can take place 'on the job', individually and in groups. It can take place outside the school such as in other schools, in professional development centres and in higher education institutions. It can be a one-off narrowly focused experience; for example, learning how to teach a particular lesson better. It can be a long-term goal perhaps leading to accreditation.

Learning on the job

There are many opportunities to learn on the job:

- reflecting on what happened in lessons
- asking the pupils their opinion of the lesson
- pupil tracking
- inviting a colleague to observe a lesson
- observing a colleague's lesson
- giving/receiving coaching from a colleague
- job shadowing a colleague
- discussions with colleagues
- team teaching
- discussions with other professionals; for example, psychologists, education social workers
- discussions with parents
- and where they still exist, inviting advisory teachers to work alongside classroom teachers.

Staff, team, department and pastoral meetings can be used for learning as well as administration as in the English department at Mill Hill County High, a secondary school in Barnet:

> Each half term department meetings are set aside to discuss teaching and learning. One such discussion around the concern that some students did not contribute to whole-class oral work, resulted in a policy of naming students to answer questions rather than relying on vociferous volunteers.
> (Myers, 1996b, p. 6)

In the same school staff have agreed to meet outside school hours:

> Mandy (the head of department) has taken advantage of the new clause in
> the recent pay and conditions document which allows teachers to be paid
> for working at weekends; twice the department has spent a Saturday at a
> local hotel reviewing and revising schemes of work.
>
> (Myers, 1996b, p. 6)

The amount we can learn from each other is often underestimated. Good
practice exists in most schools, yet inservice sessions often consist of
bringing in the 'expert' from outside. We are certainly not 'knocking'
this practice because an outsider's perspective can be very useful.
However, inviting teachers within the school to share their experience
with colleagues can underline the notion that good practice is valued and
acknowledged in the school. Moreover, having to make a presentation
to colleagues can in itself be a good learning experience.

Teacher action research

Teacher action research can be an invaluable method of learning on the
job. It involves addressing an issue in a systematic way. The research
issue chosen is one that is identified by those involved as in need of
attention.

The typical action research cycle involves:

- identifying the issue
- auditing what is already happening
- planning a piece of development work
- implementing the action
- reviewing what has happened
- replanning the next step.

Action research can be an individual activity. For example, a teacher
may want to discover the differences between male and female contributions in her lessons. Having identified the research issue, she would then
plan how to obtain this information. The plan would include the number
of lessons to be involved in the study, which classes, the time of day/
week and the means of collecting data – for example, by using a tape
recorder and observation. The action in this case would be collecting the
data. Once collected and analysed, the teacher would replan based on
her findings. If she found, for example, that some girls rarely volunteered
to contribute to whole-class discussion but were quite vociferous in
group work, she would decide whether this was an issue to pursue and
then if necessary devise a plan to tackle it. Her plan would start the cycle
again.

Pursuing action research individually, however, can be lonely and
frustrating and may become disconnected from the rest of the school.

The teacher in this situation may also be unaware of, and consequently unable to learn from, other research and experience on the issue being addressed. We believe that teacher action research is most beneficial when it includes groups of teachers or even a whole school. When this happens opportunities for collaboration, sharing findings, analysing results and planning future developments can be exciting and invigorating for those involved. Those involved are also much more likely to believe in and consequently carry out any change suggested because of their participation in the process.

To be useful, teacher action research like all other research must be rigorous and evidence-based. (See McMahon, 1993, for advice on how to proceed.) The work can be accredited as part of a diploma or masters course. Schools can also use institutes of higher education to provide school-based inset on action research, to inform teachers about published research on the issue being addressed, to put teachers in touch with others involved in similar initiatives and for external evaluation purposes. The TTA has acknowledged the importance of teacher action research and has made funds available to support some initiatives.

Learning outside the school

Learning that takes place outside the school should be seen as complementary to the learning described above. Many schools now use inservice training days as an opportunity to arrange joint sessions with colleagues from other schools. This can be cost-effective and has the advantage of facilitating and encouraging cross-fertilisation of ideas without necessitating raiding the supply budget. There are times, though, when it is worth financing visits to other schools to observe the practice of other teachers. On a school improvement project that one of us was involved in, taking groups of heads and senior staff to visit other schools proved to be an invaluable experience:

> Where possible we travelled together and the ensuing conversation on the forward and return journeys provided opportunities to discuss educational issues in general and what we had seen in particular. Without exception, host schools were generous – both with their time and the sharing of ideas. They were pleased that the work they were doing was being acknowledged, valued and appreciated and said they found the visits stimulating. We found the visits one of the most beneficial forms of inservice experience we had undergone and several . . . initiatives were adopted and adapted from initiatives we had observed.
>
> (Myers, 1996c, p. 53)

As well as visiting other schools, teachers can take advantage of courses and seminars run by centres for professional development and higher education (HE) institutions. There are good examples across the country of partnerships between LEAs, HE and schools that encourage professional development. ISEIC, for example, has recently been involved in a 'Leadership for Learning' course jointly designed with Lambeth LEA. The course enables primary headteachers to have the opportunity to review and plan how they can be both the headteacher and the head learner. Many schools now have close working relationships with HE centres that are partners in initial teacher training and these relationships can be extended to support teachers' inservice development. One example of this support is providing mentor training for school-based professional tutors. At the Institute of Education, University of London, professional tutors are offered a range of support in mentoring including school and institute-based accredited courses, subject-related support and consultancy provision.

We have discussed why teachers need to learn and where learning opportunities can exist. Jennifer Nias and colleagues (1992) found that teachers who wanted to improve their practice were characterised by four attitudes:

1. they accepted it was possible to improve
2. they were ready to be self-critical
3. they were ready to recognise better practice than their own in school and elsewhere
4. they were willing to learn what had to be learned to be able to do what had to be done.

Promoting and encouraging these attitudes is fundamental to encouraging teachers' learning.

Encouraging learning

Motivation in teacher learning

Surveys of teacher morale (Sutcliffe, 1997) and numbers opting for early retirement suggest that teacher morale is fairly low at the time of writing. Being constantly told by the media and some official sources that everything teachers do is inadequate is not conducive to improving morale. And since morale and motivation are linked (Varlaam, Nuttall and Walker, 1992) it is vital that steps are taken to improve this situation. The issue is acknowledged by the TTA but needs to be addressed elsewhere too.

At school level, the literature on school improvement suggests that teachers need to find both meaning and 'ownership' in order to want to participate in change efforts. Encouraging motivation is a challenge for all managers but we know from various studies that workers are more likely to feel involved and motivated if they are treated in particular ways. The 'Hawthorne studies' that took place in the 1920s are probably the most famous example of this (Mayo, 1930). In this study the women workers improved their output whatever the extrinsic changes that were made to their working conditions – for example, increasing or decreasing light. It appeared that involving them in the decision-making process about the changes proposed was much more important than the changes themselves. Susan Rosenholtz's research (1989) characterises schools that encourage 'ownership' as 'learning enriched' and 'moving'. In the 'learning impoverished' or 'stuck' schools which have no such ethos, she found that teachers were more likely not to take personal responsibility for what was happening, blamed others and were too isolated from each other to share in any mutual enterprise of learning.

Earlier in this chapter we mentioned opportunities for teachers to learn on the job. Most of them involve working collaboratively with colleagues. Roland Barth (1990) distinguishes between congeniality (being nice to each other) and collegiality (working together to improve practice). He believes that a number of outcomes may be associated with collegiality:

> Decisions tend to be better. Implementation of decisions is better. There is a higher level of trust and morale among adults. *Adult learning is energized and more likely to be sustained.* There is even some evidence that motivation of students and their achievements rises, and evidence that when adults share and co-operate, students do the same.
>
> (Barth, 1990, p. 31, emphasis added)

We develop the theme of collegial *intelligence* in the final chapter.

Roland Barth also refers to the crucial role of headteachers in this process. As mentioned in Chapter 1, he believes they should be seen as the head learner (Barth, 1990, p. 46) and emphasises the importance of their behaviour in connection with modelling and passing on implicit and explicit messages to pupils and staff. In this way heads set a climate conducive to learning for both adults and pupils.

When we invited schools and LEAs to share with us their strategies for school improvement to use in this book, we received a range of different examples to illustrate how teachers working collaboratively are also learning collaboratively.

Working and learning together

It seems that working collaboratively is taken very seriously at Brunswick Park Infants School in Camberwell. Teachers are paired together in terms of experience, strengths and interests in classrooms that have been deliberately opened up so that teachers can work together and share their practice. Staff also work in curriculum teams covering arts, sciences and humanities so that expertise can be shared within these teams. They aim to incorporate action research principles into their appraisal system so that it will become self-managing and supportive without losing rigour.

The Secondary Team Leader of the Pupil Development Support Service in Rochdale described working with a senior teacher and her colleagues in Queen Elizabeth High School. The object of the initiative was to improve standards of literacy by raising teachers' awareness of the issues and equipping teachers in all departments with practical strategies. School-based inservice sessions on the teaching of reading using practical, fun tasks were offered to all staff. They worked together and learned together to raise pupils' achievement. According to the writer, all the children involved in the initiative made significant progress – a good example of teachers' and children's learning being inextricably linked.

At Avondale Park Primary School in Kensington and Chelsea, encouraging an 'observation culture' has been central to teachers' learning about their own teaching. Teachers are regularly observed by both the head and deputy but on different days and times. The criteria for these observations (based on the school development plan and the teaching and learning policy), are discussed, debated and agreed with the whole staff. Teachers complete a pre-observation sheet and feedback is given within a week. Teachers are also encouraged to observe each other using targets that have been set during the monitoring feedback. We are told that a supportive culture for monitoring has been established through a careful discussion of the process and establishing the information needed by the teachers. By having clearly agreed criteria about the nature of effective teaching, classroom processes are actively influenced and improved.

Staff meetings are an opportunity to learn from each other at Haslemere First School, in Mitcham. Weekly meetings are held on a rota basis in everyone's classroom. The first ten minutes of the staff meeting are dedicated to the focus area and the class teacher of the particular classroom discusses his/her ways of developing this area of the curriculum. Display, practical teaching strategies, organisation of the class for the curriculum area and examples of children's work are discussed and shared.

Teachers at Fulham Cross Secondary School in Hammersmith and Fulham have established ways for academic and pastoral staff to learn from each other by working together. PACTS (academic and pastoral teams) have developed and, at the time of writing, the school is piloting an Academic Profile for each student. The information is collected by the form tutor and discussed with students at regular intervals. In addition, these teams have developed a range of strategies to promote better classroom and behaviour management.

A range of procedures to support the teaching process and the teacher have been established at Churchfield Primary School in Edmonton. One strategy is encouraging subject managers to visit other schools in the partnership group in order to observe organisation and practice in a different context.

Jennifer Nias and colleagues (1992, p. 93) report that teachers and headteachers see professional learning as the key to developing the curriculum and the main way to school improvement. They discovered that:

> Teachers, like other adult learners, found some means of learning more congenial and more effective than others. The success of the opportunities to learn, provided, promoted and used by headteachers and others depended in part on how they were carried out. We found that teachers appeared to make particularly productive use of four types of activity: talk, observation, practice and reflection.

The examples we have quoted give the teachers involved opportunities to do all four of these types of activity. They highlight some of the issues referred to in Chapter 2 where we discussed metacognition – thinking about thinking (see page 22—3). In that chapter we emphasised the importance of allowing learners to feel a sense of ownership over what they are learning and giving them occasions to process this learning. Providing these opportunities is an important part of the teachers' job whether the learners are adults or children.

Adults other than teachers

This chapter has addressed the learning needs of teachers but of course others involved with schools have learning needs too, in particular, support staff and governors. Haslemere First School, for example, is fortunate enough to have a classroom assistant in each class. Their learning needs are taken as seriously as those of the teachers. They have termly training sessions and participate in all the major decisions taken in the school. In the same school, governors' training needs are addressed by offering joint staff/governor training sessions. These sessions have encouraged trust and understanding between the two groups and recently led to the production of a governor visiting policy. According to the head:

> It was the joint training to devise the policy that resulted in governors and staff talking openly about their respective worries over the formal visiting process.

Greenvale Special School in Lewisham has an annual two-day residential conference for all teaching and support staff and the governors. This provides an opportunity for everyone to review, evaluate and learn about new developments in the school. The focus for the 1995 conference was practical approaches to improving practice in classrooms. In 1996 the discussion centred around the development of the humanities curriculum for students with profound and severe learning difficulties. The evaluation by governors of this conference revealed that all of them found it to be a worthwhile experience. As one governor said: 'It enabled me to have a better understanding of how the various subjects are taught in school.'

Parents have a part to play in this process as well. Some schools such as Haggerston Secondary School in Hackney have offered family classes; for example, in literacy. This gives parents the opportunity to learn alongside their offspring. Other schools, for example Anfield Community School in Liverpool, have, in partnership with their local further education provider, offered opportunities for parents' work in the classroom to be accredited through their 'parents as educators project'. Some parents have used this accreditation to move on to an access course and then higher education. In the same school, parents have been able to sit in on GCSE classes and some who did not have wonderful memories of their own schooling have managed to gain qualifications and more importantly self-esteem through this opportunity.

Important messages are given to students when they see and hear about the adults they know – teachers, support staff and parents – pursuing their own learning.

Conclusion

In a recent teacher survey undertaken by MORI for the TTA (1995), about the effectiveness of professional development, 89 per cent of respondents said it was useful or very useful but only 26 per cent thought it had a great deal of impact on classroom practice. We believe that teachers' learning must ultimately make a difference for the pupils. This does not mean that all learning should be about how to organise the classroom or how, for example, to teach phonics. It does mean, however, that the learning that teachers undertake as part of their professional responsibilities should somehow and in some way enhance their teaching. This may happen through attending practical sessions on classroom organisation. It may equally happen through being enthused and excited by some recent academic research on the subject.

We have discussed the importance of teachers' learning and suggested ways it can be pursued. In all schools, there are individuals involved in some of the processes described above. In *the intelligent school*, however, it is not left to chance. There is an overview of the development needs of the staff and a plan to meet these needs. This plan contains a balance between individual, group, whole-staff, on-site, off-site, short-term and long-term needs.

The intelligent school knows why learning is so important, it provides opportunities for learning and provides opportunities for that learning to be put to good use – that is, used intelligently to maximise pupils' progress and achievement. In the next chapter we pursue this theme.

Questions for discussion

1. What opportunities for teachers' learning are available in your school? How many of these are there by chance and how many are there by design?

2. Are there opportunities for teachers' learning to be shared? How could these opportunities be improved?

3. What are the connections between learning opportunities for teachers and classroom practice?

5

Maximising pupils' progress and achievement

An effective school adds extra value to its students' outcomes in comparison with other schools serving similar intakes.

(Sammons, Hillman and Mortimore, 1995, p. 3)

In Chapter 4 we focused on teachers' learning. The underlying message was that, however effective an individual teacher might be, no one teacher on his or her own can make a school more effective. *The intelligent school* understands that whole-school effectiveness can only be achieved if teachers work together to develop the curriculum and to improve their practice. In the last chapter we identified school-wide strategies for supporting the learning of teachers. Practical ways in which teachers can share and improve their practice through learning with and from one another were described.

In this chapter we continue with the theme of learning but shift the focus back to pupils' learning and, in particular, to ways of maximising their progress and achievement. As we suggested in Chapter 4, teachers' learning and pupils' learning are inextricably linked and therefore need to be developed together. For a school to be effective, simply concentrating on supporting teachers' learning is not enough. Equally important is the need for teachers to monitor and evaluate pupils' learning and to involve them in this process, so as to be able to reflect upon the amount of progress they are making. If a teacher knows what pupils currently know and can do, then this information can be used to ensure that learning intentions in lesson plans and the teaching strategies chosen are directly related to what the pupils need to know and be able to do next.

We begin with a consideration of some of the factors that need to be taken into account when focusing on pupils' progress and achievement. To do this we draw together some of the key themes identified in the previous four chapters. We then describe three different types of evidence schools gather to find out about pupils' progress and achievement and how schools use this evidence to set specific targets for

improvement. Strategies to gather evidence and set targets are illustrated with examples of what some schools and LEAs have done. The chapter concludes with a detailed description of how two schools have managed to ensure that teaching and learning in the classroom are at the heart of their improvement efforts.

Focusing on pupil progress and outcomes

Drawing on some of the themes developed in the first four chapters, there are at least four key issues schools need to take into account when focusing on the progress that pupils make and on their learning outcomes. These concern:

- the relationship between pupil progress and the extent to which a school can be deemed to be effective

- our knowledge about learners and their learning

- the need for staff development to be linked with pupil development

- lessons learnt from studies of schools seeking to improve themselves.

The relationship between pupil progress and the extent to which a school can be deemed to be effective

In Chapter 1 we explained the importance of a school being able to assess the amount of progress pupils make from year to year. As part of this explanation we issued a health warning in respect of the caution needed when using and interpreting raw data and value-added tables (see pages 1–4). We then explored the potential use and usefulness of value-added measures not least because there is an abundance of research evidence to show that

> all other things being equal, disadvantaged students as a group are less likely to do well those from advantaged backgrounds . . . Accordingly, measures of progress are needed which can take account of the students' initial starting points.
>
> (Mortimore, 1993, p. 297)

Such measures of individual pupils' progress can do at least three things. They can demonstrate over time whether or not there is an upward or downward trend in pupils' achievements. They can demonstrate whether or not there is school-wide, key stage or year group high or low achievement compared with the pupils' starting points. They can also demonstrate that some individual or groups of pupils may have done better or less well than might have been expected. For example, the same pupils may have achieved very differently across a range of subjects

(O'Donoghue *et al.*, 1997, Sammons, Thomas and Mortimore, 1997). Similarly, as described in Chapter 2, pupils of a particular gender or ethnic group may have achieved less well than their peers (Gillborn and Gipps, 1996). There will be different reasons for this. The reliability of the statistical data may well be an issue (Goldstein, 1996). High achievement in some areas may be the result of the teaching being of a better quality in some subjects or some classes compared with others. Low achievement could be the result of low expectations. It could be the result of complacency on behalf of the school. It could be the result of poor teaching. It could be the result of poor levels of motivation amongst the pupils. It could be the result of factors beyond the control of the school. The point is that having gathered evidence about pupil progress and achievement, the staff can then have a rigorous, focused debate about the effectiveness of the teaching provision in the classroom and about the effectiveness of the school as a whole in relation to the intake of pupils. According to Peter Mortimore (1996, p. 3):

> an effective school regularly promotes the highest academic and other achievement for the maximum number of its students regardless of the socio-economic backgrounds of their families.

When considering its effectiveness *the intelligent school* takes account of the eleven characteristics of effectiveness listed in Chapter 1, not least because eight of these have a direct link with pupils' learning as the modified extract in Table 5.1, from a booklet published for governors (DFE/Ofsted, 1995), illustrates.

Each of these features has an important role to play in promoting pupils' achievement but on their own are unlikely to make much difference. What effective schools have learnt to do is to bring these features together in such a way that the school does 'add extra value to its students' outcomes in comparison with other schools serving similar intakes' (Sammons, Hillman and Mortimore, 1995, p. 3).

Our knowledge about learners and their learning

In Chapter 2 we emphasised that learners come in different shapes and sizes and have different learning needs and preferred learning styles. We argued that for learning to take place the learner must want to learn and believe that she is capable of doing well. We also stressed the powerful influence of teachers' expectations and how the way a pupil is taught has an important influence on the learning that takes place.

Any assessment of pupil progress and achievement therefore needs to take these factors into consideration. Such an assessment must bear in mind the quality and the range of learning opportunities that are being

Table 5.1 Features of effective schools that have a direct link with pupils' learning

1. *A learning environment*
   The school provides a climate in which pupils are able and willing to learn. The atmosphere is orderly and purposeful, and the working environment is attractive.

2. *Concentrating on teaching and learning*
   The school's activities have one central purpose – helping pupils to learn and to achieve.

3. *Explicit high expectations*
   The school has high expectations of what pupils can achieve. These are communicated clearly to all pupils, and lessons are intellectually challenging.

4. *Positive reinforcement*
   Discipline is clear and fair. Staff make sure that pupils know how they are doing and take particular care to praise them for good work.

5. *Monitoring progress*
   Staff systematically monitor and evaluate the achievements of pupils, and of the school as a whole.

6. *Pupil rights and responsibilities*
   The school promotes pupils' self-esteem. It encourages them to take responsibility, particularly for their own work.

7. *Purposeful teaching*
   The quality of teaching is high, particularly because: lessons are efficiently organised; they have a clear purpose and are well structured; and the teaching takes account of the fact that different pupils learn in different ways.

8. *Home–school partnership*
   Relations between home and school are supportive and co-operative. Parents get actively involved in their children's work and in the life of the school.

Source: from DFE/Ofsted, 1995, p. 1.

provided for different kinds of pupils and for different purposes and that these affect the quality of the learning outcomes achieved.

The need for staff development to be linked with pupil development

Supporting teachers' continuous professional development is essential as we argued in Chapter 4. The ultimate aim of improving teaching effectiveness must be to improve pupil progress and achievement. Therefore, a planned programme of staff development to improve the quality of teaching throughout the school needs to establish a direct link with pupil development.

To achieve this aim, teachers need to know about the quality and effectiveness of teaching and learning beyond their own classroom. In the words of Hopkins (1989), teachers need to develop a 'classroom exceeding perspective'. They need to know about standards of achievement across a year group, a key stage, a department, and the school as a whole in order to be able to judge how well their pupils are doing. At the same time, headteachers, senior staff and postholders need to acquire a 'classroom perceiving perspective' (MacGilchrist *et al.*, 1995). In other words, they need to know what is happening in individual classrooms in order to be able to assess the quality and effectiveness of the teaching and learning taking place. Chapter 4 provided a range of examples as to how this can be achieved.

When the headteacher and the staff bring these two kinds of information together they are in a strong position to make judgements about where improvements in practice are needed. These judgements can then give a sense of purpose and direction to the staff development programme. In this way, inservice activities can be explicitly linked to strategies for improving the quality of teaching and learning and maximising pupil progress and achievement. In this way staff development no longer remains an act of faith. Instead, adult learning is linked directly with pupils' learning.

Lessons learnt from studies of schools seeking to improve themselves

As explained in Chapter 1, school improvement researchers stress, as we have just done, the importance of making the link between school development, teacher development and classroom practice (Fullan, Bennett and Rolheiser-Bennett, 1990). A good illustration of this key issue are the findings of the recent study of the impact of development planning (MacGilchrist *et al.*, 1995) conducted by one of us which were described in the first chapter.

There was only one type of plan – the *corporate* plan - which was found to make a link between development at the level of the whole school, teacher development and increased opportunities for pupils' learning in the classroom. This was because everyone in the school – hence the word corporate – was commited to improving pupils' progress and achievement. Pupils' learning was being systematically monitored and evaluated. Evidence was being gathered about pupils' progress and then used as the starting point for the identification of priorities for improvement which were then built into the school development plan. The staff development programme focused on these priorities and was rooted therefore in classroom practice.

Similar lessons can be learnt from other school improvement initiatives. For example, improvement projects have been funded through the government's Grants for Educational Support and Training (GEST) scheme. In 1993/4 funding was made available for programmes to raise standards of literacy in schools. The evaluation of the success of these schemes (DFE, 1994, p. 7) makes interesting reading. The main findings were as follows.

All enjoyed at least 'modest success', but all succeeded in:

- raising awareness of the need for change
- stimulating interest of teachers
- on occasion, stimulating interest of parents.

Many had achieved:

- raising quality of teaching and
- raising self-esteem of pupils.

A few had managed to raise standards.

For many of these projects, therefore, the pupils' progress and outcomes were the missing link. The message was that insufficient attention had been paid to the identification of specific targets for improvement related to the pupils' own learning.

The lessons learnt from the first wave of post-Ofsted inspection action plans (Ofsted, 1995, p. 4) further confirm the need for improvement efforts to be much more sharply focused. An analysis of the plans revealed that whilst two-fifths of the schools were managing plans and improvements well, few:

- set specific targets for improvement of achievement (4 per cent)
- had developed criteria or indicators against which to monitor and evaluate the effectiveness of the proposed action in terms of raised standards (8 per cent).

To be able to set specific targets requires detailed information about pupils' progress and achievements. The next section describes practical ways in which such information can be obtained.

Finding out about pupil progress and achievement

To make a judgement about the progress and achievements of individual pupils and groups of pupils *the intelligent school* knows it needs to do at least three things:

- Find out about what pupils know and can do when they first begin at the school. In other words, gather 'base-line' information.
- Find out about pupils' progress in the classroom. In other words, obtain a 'classroom perceiving' perspective.
- Compare pupils' achievements in different ways using school, local and national data. In other words, obtain a 'classroom and a school exceeding' perspective.

In this way the school draws upon and combines some of the intelligences we describe in the final chapter.

What follows are examples of the ways in which some schools have accomplished these tasks. We are not advocating the examples as blueprints to be copied. We have simply chosen them because they represent the kinds of practical strategies that schools have adopted that best suit their context.

'Base-line' information – finding out about what pupils know and can do when they first begin at a school

Without 'base-line' data it is not possible to assess the progress a pupil is making or to make a judgement about what that pupil manages to achieve. Nor is it possible to know whether or not the school itself is particularly effective compared with other schools with a similar intake locally or nationally. Some caution is needed, however, when using base-line data. For example, the pupils themselves may well make progress despite, rather than because of, the school (Myers, 1995). Also, as Schagen (1997, p. 14) points out:

> If a school either in reality or through some technique which 'massages' the results, achieves above average results for its pupils at the end of one stage, then those pupils have to produce even better scores at the next stage for a good value-added result.

In other words, much depends on the reliabity of the base-line data collected.

Secondary schools have traditionally been better placed than primary schools to gather this kind of evidence. In the past they tended to receive variable information from feeder schools and there was a general scepticism among primary teachers about the notice that was taken of information passed on. Given the increased accountability of schools and, in particular, the widespread acceptance of the importance of demonstrating the value-added by a school, secondary schools now tend to take much more notice of the evidence they receive. The nature of that evidence has also changed. It now tends to be less *ad hoc* and to include statistical data about an individual pupil's academic achievements and qualitative information about, for example, their particular learning needs, their attitudes to learning, attendance, behaviour and interpersonal relationships. This has enabled secondary schools to be in a stronger position to identify the particular learning needs of any given intake.

Another quite common means of transferring information from one school to the next is through the use of a 'pupil portfolio' in which the pupil has selected, with the help of teachers, exemplars of best work. 'Records of Achievement' are also quite commonplace although, regrettably, the use of a National Record of Achievement (NRA) has not become the norm across the country. As well as these kinds of records many secondary schools still feel the need to supplement transfer information with their own test procedures, in particular the setting of reading, numeracy and cognitive ability tests.

It has only been in recent years, as described in Chapter 1, that most primary schools now recognise and accept the need to gather information about children in a much more structured and rigorous way when they first begin school. The findings of research are proving helpful in making primary base-line assessment more focused. For example, a colleague of ours at the Institute has recently published her research findings about the relationship between young children's knowledge of reading on entry to school and their progress twelve months later (Riley, 1996, pp. 67–8). She found that, in order of importance, those children who enter the reception class with:

- a well-developed knowledge of the alphabet
- an ability to write their own names
- an understanding of the concepts about print, and
- a positive adjustment to school

have an 80 per cent chance of reading (at least in line with their chronological age) by July of the same academic year.

She also found, however, that: 'The majority of the reception classteachers surveyed ranked the importance of the entry skills in the reverse order' (pp. 67–8).

In other words, the reception classteachers in this study were not aware of the most 'predictive entry skills' and so were not in a strong position to design the most appropriate reading programme for each child. This kind of research illustrates the need to make base-line assessments of those aspects of young children's development that are most likely to have an impact on future progress and achievement.

At the time of writing, work is progressing, led by SCAA, on a national framework for base-line assessment. In the mean time more than half of the LEAs in the country, along with some other agencies, have developed their own schemes. Table 5.2 provides an extract from a 'base-line checklist' developed by Wandsworth LEA which is supported by a detailed Handbook.

Schools using this particular checklist do so when children enter the reception class usually just before the half-term break in the term that they are admitted. The information recorded is obtained from teacher assessments, a conference with the child's parent(s) or guardian and from test data. Included in the checklist is a Linguistic Awareness and Reading Readiness (LARR) test. Each school sends the LEA the raw

Table 5.2 Base-line checklist for science

					Score (see Key)
1	Makes observations of familiar materials and communicates these observations	1	2	3	
2	Asks how, what and why questions	1	2	3	
3	Talks about the characteristics of living things	1	2	3	
4	Identifies materials: (circle as appropriate) metal glass wood plastic paper fabric/cloth	NO		YES	
5	Identifies materials or objects that are hard/soft				
				TOTAL	

Source: Wandsworth LEA.

pupil results and these are analysed and sent back in a form that enables a school to identify the differential performance of pupils and to decide what action needs to be taken. For example, as a result of receiving this information Allfarthing JMI School in the Borough has been able to focus on specific needs of individual children at the pre-reading stage.

A 'classroom perceiving perspective' – finding out about pupils' progress in the classroom

The kinds of evidence a school gathers to find out about pupils' learning in the classroom will depend on the individual or group to be studied and the purpose for which the data are being collected. Sometimes the focus might be tracking the academic or personal and social development of an individual pupil. Sometimes the focus might be the progress of a particular group of pupils in a class, a subject area or perhaps a year group. The purpose could be to observe the effectiveness of the teaching in a curriculum area or it could be to assess, for example, whether or not the school's policy on teaching and learning is being implemented. Schools, therefore, need to be clear as to who or what is the focus of attention, why they want to collect the information and what they intend to do with it.

Schools collect two main types of evidence, namely quantitative and qualitative data. Both are useful, complement each other and can be used simultaneously. The issue for schools is to decide which type of evidence is most appropriate for the purpose in hand. Using quantitative measures such as value-added test or examination scores for an individual pupil provides an important means of assessing individual progress. It also enables comparisons to be made between one pupil's results and another's or between groups of pupils. The reader is reminded again, however, of the health warning in Chapter 1 about using such data (see pages 1–4). Attendance figures, behaviour records and homework completion rates are further examples of the kinds of evidence that can also be quantified.

As important is the collection and use of qualitative data which requires perceptive judgements to be made about pupil progress and outcomes and the quality of teaching. When such evidence is collected in a carefully controlled way, it too can lend itself to some form of quantifiable 'measure'. Increasingly, schools and external support agencies have been developing a range of strategies for gathering different types of qualitative evidence. The most common forms of evidence used are:

- *visual*, i.e. going into classrooms and observing what is happening
- *documentary*, i.e. collecting different kinds of written information
- *people's perceptions*, i.e. talking to people including, of course, the pupils and surveying their views.

Observing in the classroom can take many forms, be for different purposes and therefore be done from different perspectives. It may involve the tracking of individual pupils by class teachers or perhaps the head of department. It could take the form of senior managers and curriculum co-ordinators looking to see if school-wide policies are being put into practice. It may concern peer review to improve an aspect of teaching or observing the work of teachers across a year group or department. It could involve looking from an equal opportunities perspective at the effectiveness and impact on the pupils of different teaching strategies such as whole-class and group techniques.

Similarly, written evidence can also take many forms and be gathered for different reasons. Examples of types of evidence we know schools find helpful include: teachers' lesson plans and their pupil records; individual pupil portfolios, 'best work' books and other samples of work; merit marks; detention notes; homework diaries; and inspection reports.

When it comes to evidence about people's perceptions our experience is that more and more schools are recognising the importance and usefulness of this source of information. It can be collected from different interest groups in different ways such as: pupil, teacher, governor and parent surveys and interviews; combined parent and pupil

Allfarthing JMI School
Summary of Tests and Assessments KS1

Nursery	Admission notes	All to next teacher.
	Individual notes	
	Work samples as	
	appropriate	
	Nursery records	
	Cumulative records	
	SEN notes	
Reception	Base-line assessment	All to next teacher.
	Individual notes	Copies of base-line to
	N.C. class book	Deputy Head.
	Cumulative records	Copies of special needs
	Special needs notes	notes to special needs
	Reading fluency sheet	co-ordinator.
	Maths check sheet	
Year 1	Individual notes	All to next teacher.
	N.C. class book	Spelling and reading
	Cumulative records	ages on sheet attached
	Reading fluency sheet	to new class record
	Maths check sheet	book.
	Reading test	Copies to Department Head
	Spelling test	and language co-ordinator,
	Special needs notes	next teacher and special
	including IEPs	needs co-ordinator.
	Sound checklists	
Year 2	Individual notes	All to next teacher.
	N.C. class book	Spelling and reading
	Cumulative records	ages in N.C. book.
	Reading fluency sheet	
	Maths check sheet	
	Special needs notes	Next teacher and
	including IEPs	special needs co-
	Sound checklists	ordinator.
	SAT results	
		On report to parents.
		Reported to Authority.
		Copies to next teacher,
		Deputy Head and subject
		co-ordinators.

Summary of Tests and Assessments KS2

Year 3	Non-Verbal Reasoning Test	Deputy Head, subject co-ordinators and next teacher.
	Individual notes	All to next teacher.
	Cumulative records	
	N.C. class records	
	Reading fluency sheet	
	Reading, spelling, and NFER Maths test	Results in N.C. class record book. Copies to
	Sound checklists	Deputy Head and subject co-ordinators.
Year 4	Individual notes	As above
	Cumulative records	
	N.C. class records	
	Reading fluency sheet	
	Reading, spelling and Maths NFER test	
	Sound checklists	
	Year 4 LEA English + maths tests	
	Richmond Test of Basic Skills Level I	
Year 5	As above, except Richmond Test of Basic Skills Level 2	As above
Year 6	Reading fluency sheet	
	Maths check sheet	
	Cumulative records	To parents.
	Individual notes	To next school.
	Modbury	
	Reading, spelling tests	
	Wandsworth tests	To Authority.
	Non-verbal reasoning	Copy to Deputy Head
	Maths	and subject co-ordinator.
	English	
	KS2 SATs	To Authority, copy to Deputy Head. **On report to parents.**
	Special Needs notes	To special needs co-ordinator.

All appropriate records are transferred to each child's secondary school.

Source: Allfarthing JMI school

conferences; staff meetings; staff appraisal; and feedback from inspectors and consultants.

Normally schools use a variety of techniques to monitor progress, record achievements and identify those pupils in need of targeted action. What follows are some examples of the range of techniques and procedures individual schools have found helpful to find out about pupils' learning.

We are not offering these examples as *the* way of doing things. We are simply describing the different ways in which real schools are going about this task. We have noticed with some of the primary examples that qualitative evidence about pupils' progress and achievement is being supplemented by test data, particularly in relation to the core subjects of English and Mathematics. Given the publication of SATs results, inspection reports and the new statutory requirement from 1998 for each school to publish targets, the increased use of tests throughout the primary years is not surprising. The challenge for schools is how to use test data intelligently.

Once evidence about pupils' progress has been gathered, *The intelligent school* reflects on this evidence and uses it to 'feedback' into plans to improve the quality of teaching and learning in the classroom. More often than not no one type of evidence on its own can provide sufficient information to enable a school to identify a specific area for improvement.

Allfarthing JMI School mentioned earlier has developed a very detailed assessment policy which includes the regular monitoring of teachers' and pupils' work. The policy involves a range of strategies for gathering evidence about pupils and their learning:

(a) Regular testing and assessment from nursery to year 6. On pages 74–6 is a summary of the tests and assessments used across Key Stages 1 and 2 and a description of what is done with the information.

(b) Teachers have an assessment focus on their weekly plans.

(c) Cumulative records and work samples are kept from 3 to 11 years.

(d) There is an individual 'Progress Chart' for each child which records certain tests and assessments.

(e) An NFER abstract reasoning test is given in year 3 to identify underachievement.

(f) Notes on special needs, including IEPs, are kept.

Christ Church Primary School
KEY PRINCIPLES OF ASSESSMENT

Assessment should show clearly what a child knows, understands and can do.

- Teacher assessment should have clear aims and inform future teaching
- It should be part of the teaching and learning process
- It should take place in familiar surroundings
- Children should know what is expected of them and what they are being assessed on
- It should be recorded in a clear and concise way to inform future planning
- Procedures should be varied and allow for different approaches to assessment, e.g. samples, testing, observing, conferencing
- It should involve looking at the 'whole child', their personal and social development, attitudes to work and each other

RECORD-KEEPING
KEY PRINCIPLES OF ASSESSMENT

Records should:

Be clear, concise and easy to maintain
Be easy to interpret
Show what an individual child has learnt and understood
Give information about the levels children are working within in relation to the national curriculum
Be accessible to parents and children
Have a common format throughout the school

Christ Church Primary School in Chelsea has developed a very comprehensive combined 'Planning, Assessment and Record-Keeping Policy' which provides teachers with practical guidelines and pro-formas for putting the policy into practice. The complete policy is described in the last section of this chapter. For the purpose of this section the extracts above from the policy describe the principles of assessment and record-keeping agreed by all the staff. The extracts on pp 78–9 describe the procedures to be used to put the principles into practice.

Haslemere First School in Mitcham has devised a system for involving pupils in improving their own progress and achievement and for taking account of their views about themselves as learners. They have a system of 'Best Work Books' which the headteacher describes as follows:

> From the nursery throughout the school examples of 'Best Work' are put into a 'Best Work Book' with comments from the teacher. In consultation with the class teacher, children select work that represents a lot of effort,

ASSESSMENT AND RECORDING
BASE-LINE ASSESSMENT – RECEPTION CLASS

This takes place when children enter the Reception Class and is carried out just before the half-term break in the term that they are admitted. It consists of a Reading Test as well as Teacher Assessment in Maths and English and a commentary on the child's social development.

PARENT CONFERENCES

These are arranged by the Reception Class teacher for children coming into the Reception Class and enable parents and teachers to exchange observations and information on the child's personal and academic development. They may also occur at other times in a child's school life, at the request of the teachers or parents.

READING PROFILES – KEY STAGES 1 & 2

These are structured assessment/recording sheets to assist in the teaching of reading and the recording of a child's achievement across the Reading Curriculum.

KEY STAGE 1 SATS – (YEAR 2)

In conjunction with the Teacher Assessments, children in year 2 will be tested in English (reading, spelling and writing including handwriting) and maths.

KEY STAGE 2 SATS – (YEAR 6)

In conjunction with Teacher Assessments, children in year 6 will be tested in English (reading, writing, spelling and handwriting), maths and science.

TEACHER ASSESSMENTS

In-house Teacher Assessment is on-going. It informs planning at all levels. It includes marking, observation of the child, dialogue with the child, and use of tasks and tests to judge individual achievement.
Teacher Assessment (TA) is a statutory requirement when a teacher is required to assess a child in core areas at the end of a Key Stage using the Level Descriptions in those areas. It has equal status with test/task results at KS 1/2.

YEAR-ON-YEAR TESTING

Pupils in years 3, 4 and 5 will be tested annually using national curriculum test materials in order to inform receiving teachers, co-ordinators and the senior management team for evaluation and monitoring purposes.

END-OF-YEAR TEACHER ASSESSMENTS

Currently used for English, maths and science, these provide information for the next year teacher and the Head/Deputy for monitoring/sampling purposes.

ANNUAL REPORT TO PARENTS

This is completed each year by the class teacher for each child. It is discussed with the parents and child and a copy is kept in the pupil's record. (Years 2 and 6 will also have SATS results included with their annual report.)

LONDON READING TEST (YEAR 6)

This is carried out in the autumn term in year 6. The results are collected by the Education Authority and also used in reporting to secondary schools.

NELSON READING/COMPREHENSION TEST

This is used by the school with particular reference to children identified as having Special Educational Needs in terms of literacy development.

FORWARDING REPORT TO SECONDARY SCHOOLS

This offers a sketch of a year 6 pupil to the receiving school and may be used for interview/tutor group purposes.

HEAD/DEPUTY MONITORING

The Head/Deputy carry out classroom observations, classroom visits, reading surveys, work sampling and structured management meetings to track achievement throughout the school.

SCHOOL PORTFOLIO

This serves as an exemplification of the standards agreed by staff in maths, science and English in the school and is a reference point for all teachers, inspectors, students, etc. when assessing achievement in the school.

Source: Christ Church Primary School

or significant improvement. Each academic year three or four pieces of work are put into the book. When children leave the school they are presented with their 'Best Work Book' as a memento of their time and achievement at the school. This process involves the children in selection of good work and recognition of their progress and achievement.

Avondale Park Primary School (see Ch. 4) uses classroom observation as one of the key ways of improving the quality of teaching and learning across the school. The headteacher described the methods used which the school has found to be successful:

We set criteria for the observations which are drawn from our Teaching and Learning Policy, as well as from targets in our School Development Plan. The criteria and related issues are discussed and debated with the staff as a whole before we observe every teacher using the agreed criteria. Teachers complete a pre-observation sheet – these change from time to time depending on the experience of staff/our past focus.

My deputy and I see the same teacher during the same week, on different days and at different times, unless the observation dictates that we see a specific session. Usually we negotiate with the teacher the day/time we will be visiting his or her classroom, but because of the nature of our current observations, although staff know when their feedback time will be, it was agreed that we will visit their classroom anytime during that week.

We feedback to the teacher together, always during the same week of the observations, and it is particularly gratifying and validating for ourselves and the observee that we usually have very similar findings to report back, despite seeing different lessons on different days. It has also proved very useful in creating a meaningful dialogue to feedback in the teacher's classroom, where we can discuss issues of teaching and learning with evidence close at hand.

To broaden and extend the 'observation culture' throughout the school it has been part of our strategy to encourage colleagues to observe each other, and this is usually suggested in the form of a target set during the feedback session. Previously we spent a lot of time discussing with the staff the nature of effective feedback and how it could be most useful and developmental, i.e. what colleagues want from feedback, how to give and receive it, how to use the feedback/discussion and evidence observed or collected in order to raise achievement through targeting, setting success indicators, how it relates to staff development, etc.

Haggerston Secondary School in Hackney, east London has developed a means of ensuring that there is always a focus on teaching and learning. For example, they have introduced a 'Progress Review' which the head-teacher described as follows:

The Progress Review has evolved from its origins as a part of Compact monitoring in the upper school into whole-school review. It begins with a snapshot report by teachers (in addition to the statutory full profile to parents) with self-assessment and opportunity for parental comment. This is then followed up by an interview for pupils with a tutor and a member of the senior team to congratulate and encourage progress or discuss concerns. Targets are set together and recorded by the tutor and the pupil in their diary for regular monitoring and review. To maintain continuity, the senior teacher follows the class from year 7 reviewing targets annually and comparing present progress with past best. The school has found that the Progress Review proves to be a very valuable opportunity to talk in small groups and with individuals about improving teaching and learning. Pupils respond positively to this coaching and encouragement.

Chiswick Community School in west London provides a comprehensive 'Handbook' for all staff. It details, among other things, the whole-school monitoring policy and how it works in practice. Integral to this policy are 'Pupil Work Reviews' which provide a means whereby parents, pupils and teachers can work in partnership to track progress and set individual targets for improvement. The following extract from the Handbook describes these reviews:

> This procedure was introduced in Spring 1988, initially with year 11 pupils. It has since been extended to years 10, 12 and 13 although increased numbers in year groups have resulted in only a proportion of students being seen in some year groups. Additionally, there are *ad hoc* work reviews for year 7, 8 and 9 students where teachers or parents have concerns in addition to a sampling by HOYs.
>
> The work review was introduced as a means of drawing parents into partnership with teachers to support pupils in the examination years, by sharing knowledge of progress and attainment and where necessary setting targets to catch up or improve key pieces of work, or make decisions about entry for public examinations.
>
> The work review enables pupils to review progress, be praised, encouraged and supported at home and school, to achieve their best. The work review gives reviewers an opportunity to monitor the work of subjects across the year group and to follow up any problems or convey congratulations with HCAs and tutors.
>
> *Procedures and Practice*
>
> 1. Upper school work reviews are scheduled.
> 2. Reviewers are Senior Management, HOY, AHOY and tutors where appropriate.
> 3. HOY is responsible for the organisation and administration: agreeing dates and times with reviewers; identifying pupils to be reviewed; matching reviewers and pupils and inviting parents; providing documentation and briefing pupils; inviting comments from subject teachers and providing interim reports if available.
> 4. Reviewers with pupil and parent check work in all subjects, especially the key items of coursework.
> 5. The review sheet includes pupil self-evaluation and the reviewer, parent and pupil will agree a summary of progress and achievement in each subject. Targets to catch up or improve may be set and follow-up meetings arranged. If the parent cannot attend they will receive a copy of the review sheet. When the follow-up is complete the review sheet goes to HOY and pupil file.
> 6. The reviewer should follow-up any issues which have emerged with HOY, tutor, HCA or subject teacher as appropriate.
> 7. *Ad hoc* work reviews may be arranged by senior staff or HOY where there are concerns expressed by teachers or parents. Parents should be invited and a summary of findings both filed via HOY and tutor and sent to parents.

As mentioned in Chapter 4, Fulham Cross Secondary School in south west London is piloting the use of an 'Academic Profile' for each pupil. The information is gathered and collated by the Academic (Form) Tutors and retained by them. The profile is intended to show pupil progress from Key Stage 2 Primary Records through to Key Stage 4 using a range of information produced by the school's own monitoring and testing arrangements. The profile records details about course work, mock and actual examination results and any action taken, SATs scores and teacher assessment for the core subjects. It also incorporates cross-curricular monitoring which is a 'snapshot' method of monitoring pupil progress, the results of which are sent home to parents in the terms in which there are no formal written reports.

What a number of these examples have in common is that they can serve multiple purposes. They provide a structure for focusing on the quality of teaching and learning in the classroom and for monitoring and evaluating improvement initiatives. This enables classteachers to assess, record and report on the progress and achievement of individual pupils and for the pupils and their parents to be active partners in this process. At the same time, they also provide a means whereby senior managers and classteachers can, together, begin to assemble a picture of pupil progress and achievement across the school as a whole. This is the third perspective in this section.

A 'classroom and school exceeding perspective' – comparing pupils' progress and achievements in different ways within and beyond the school

When considering the need for staff development to be linked with pupil achievement, we emphasised the importance of classteachers under-standing the 'big picture' in respect of school-wide levels of achievement as well as the 'little picture' in terms of what their own pupils are achieving in the classroom. The relationship between the different parts of an organisation and the organisation as a whole is explored in Chapter 6. Knowing the 'big picture' enables classteachers to set their pupils' progress and outcomes within a wider school context and to compare or benchmark these with local and national achievement data. In the ex-amples provided in this section schools have tended to use a mix of 'home-grown' quantitative and qualitative techniques and procedures and systems devised by local authorities and other agencies.

As noted earlier, some of the procedures used to obtain a classroom perceiving perspective can also be used to acquire a school-wide picture. The evidence, however, needs to be gathered with the following sorts of questions in mind (DFE/Ofsted, 1995, p. 3, our additions emphasised).

1. How is our school currently performing?
2. Are some parts of the school more effective than others? If so, why? *What can we do about it?*
3. Are some groups of pupils doing better than others? If so, why? *What can we do about it?*
4. How does the school's achievement now compare with its previous achievement?
5. How does the school's performance compare with that of other schools? *What can we do about it?*

Much of the evidence gathered about individual pupils' learning and about the progress that particular groups make – for example, in an area of the curriculum – can be used for another purpose. It can be used to enable the school to get a picture of progress and achievement beyond an individual teacher's class or subject. It can help to provide a picture of achievement across a year group, across all the subjects in a school, across a Key Stage or across the school as a whole.

For example, raw individual pupil test data can be transformed, using value-added techniques, into data that, up to a certain level of accuracy, can tell a school how well pupils are performing year on year, how their performance compares with the LEA average, how it compares with a group of schools locally that have a similar intake and how it compares with national norms. Other statistical data about, for example, individual attendance and behaviour can also be easily converted to provide school-wide information.

Work reviews can become a general means of sampling work to assess standards and track progress. For this to be effective staff need to have reached agreement about the standard of work that is acceptable for the different levels within national curriculum subjects. Similarly, focused reviews of particular groups of pupils can take place across a section of the school or across the school as a whole. As part of this process, for example, pupils, teachers and parents can be surveyed for their views about progress and the quality of teaching and learning. Our experience is that schools find such surveys a rich source of evidence.

These and other techniques for obtaining evidence about the overall quality of teaching and learning and about overall standards are becoming well developed in more and more schools. The following provide just some examples of what schools are doing and the kinds of services external agencies are providing.

Norwood Secondary School for girls in south east London has put in place a detailed pupil monitoring system which has an identified focus for each academic year. The procedures involve senior staff and classroom teachers and a targeted group of pupils who, along with their parents or guardian, are consulted and involved in the process. The process is described below along with the agreed criteria used for monitoring pupils' work.

The introduction of monitoring this year will centre on the classroom experience of all our girls and basic requirements of homework, completion of coursework/classwork, attendance at lessons, punctuality, preparedness for lessons and appearance. Starting from half-term onwards, the following staff will be involved in monitoring in the following ways:

1. Headteacher
   - six pupils per half-term
   - interviews with pupils and parents
   - examination of all exercise books and journals
   - follow-up with appropriate staff
   - line-management meetings with Deputies and KS3 and KS4 managers

2. Deputies
   - three pupils per half-term each
   - examination of all exercise books and journals
   - line-management – meetings with HOFs/HODs
   - random checks on registers in appropriate key stage
   - random spot checks on attendance

3. KS/4 Manager
   - visit each tutor group in key stage once per term during lesson time
   - check all registers once per half-term
   - check all journals once per half-term
   - line-management meetings with HOYs once per half-term

4. HODs/HOFs
   - check classrooms for display work each half-term
   - check exercise books/registers once per half-term
   - keep records of department assessment for scrutiny by Deputy Heads and Headteacher

5. HOYs
   - check registers weekly
   - visit each tutor group on a rolling programme weekly, during tutor period
   - random checks on uniform, equipment and journals

6. Group tutors/ teachers
   - complete register each lesson
   - complete AM and PM registers and return to the office
   - follow up absence from school. Make every effort to get absence authorised
   - inform HOY of truancy
   - check and sign journals each week
   - ensure pupils carry same
   - mark work regularly and follow up incomplete work.

Criteria for monitoring pupils' work
Choose three pupils from the same form.

> One pupil of high ability.
> One pupil of average ability.
> One pupil of low ability.

Notify the parents by letter that their daughters will be the subject of monitoring to ensure high standards of teaching and learning.

Arrange time to interview pupils and parents after the monitoring is complete.

Collect a full set of exercise books and journals from pupils.

Consult pupils' files or other sources of information to get information on banding, last school report, Key Stage Test scores as appropriate.

Examine books with the following criteria in mind:

Is there evidence: – of differentiation?
 – of extension work?
 – that pupils' learning difficulties have been addressed?
 – that bilingualism has been addressed?
 – of regular, meaningful homework?
 – of regular, helpful marking?
 – of progress during the year of the life of the exercise book?

Is there an apparent variation in standards of work in different subjects?

Observe the pupils in a lesson to monitor their performance. Does it accord with evidence in the books?

Report back on monitoring:
 – positive comments to pupils and parents
 – raise concerns with HODs, KS managers, HOYs and tutors as appropriate.

Haggerston School, like Norwood, has also introduced a system for monitoring the work of faculties. It takes the form of 'Work Reviews' which the headteacher described for us:

> The Work Review focuses on each faculty in turn. There is a review of documentation and pupil work and observation of lessons. After feedback from senior staff to the faculty an action plan is devised. Faculties and senior staff are able to discuss issues of teaching and learning and develop faculty and whole-school strategies to raise achievement.

Vicarage Primary School in the London Borough of Newham examines samples of pupils' work from across the school on a regular basis. Work is collected in from four categories of pupil: above average; average; below average; and an underachieving child. It was this last category that proved to be a particularly useful catalyst for debate.

Kemnal Technology College for boys in Bromley produces an 'Educational Outcome Report Form' each year on a number of key factors that are directly or indirectly related to pupil progress and achievements. This Report enables general information to be recorded and compared year on year such as attendance, unauthorised absence and staying-on rate at age 16. It includes a summary of the results of an annual parental survey which incorporates the kinds of questions asked by inspectors during an Ofsted inspection.

The Report Form also provides detailed information about examination results and pays particular attention to the results of those pupils who received special needs tuition in their primary school. It compares subject results within school and with national averages and predicts future results. The academic progress of particular pupils who have been the subject of a personal mentoring scheme is also recorded. The Report is used by staff to identify targets for improvement the next year.

Portchester Secondary School in Bournemouth has devised a system for collecting and analysing 'Mock Examination Results'. Table 5.3 describes the process. In the next section the systems the school uses to set faculty targets and pupil targets are described.

Secondary schools around the country use different data sets to analyse their examination results. For example, through our International School Effectiveness and Improvement Centre (ISEIC), at the Institute of Education, we work in partnership with LEAs and schools, as other universities do, to provide a value-added analysis, year on year, of examination results.

In relation to SATs, West Sussex local authority is able to provide its primary and secondary schools with four types of data:

- a school's own SATs results
- the results of those schools in the authority that have a similar intake (each school has its own number so can identify the group it belongs to)
- the LEA average
- the national average.

ISEIC also offers other kinds of analyses. For example, the Institute is currently working with the University of Strathclyde on a school improvement research project (Robertson and Sammons, 1997) funded by the Scottish Education and Industry Department. As part of this research the team has developed a pupil questionnaire to enable the 80 Scottish primary and secondary schools involved to obtain the views their pupils have about the school and their own learning. The pupils are asked questions about the school in general; for example, homework, how

Table 5.3   Mock examination results – collection, analysis, action

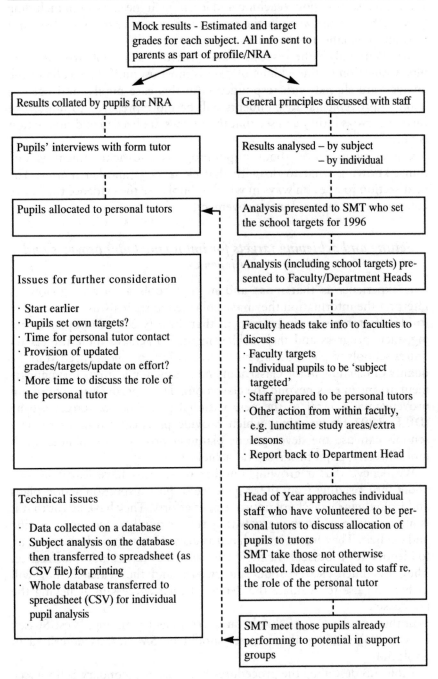

Source: Portchester School

teachers treat them and extra-curricular activities. They are also asked specific questions about teaching and learning in the classroom including how interesting the work is, the feedback they receive from teachers and how approachable teachers are.

We then analyse the responses and provide the schools with the results. Collection of these kinds of data is most useful if the results of the analysis are shared with respondents (in this case pupils) and used to make improvements. Respondents will be more prepared to undertake further surveys if they can see that their views are heeded and that action is taken.

Gathering evidence about pupil progress and achievement is one thing, knowing what to do with that evidence is another matter. The next section focuses on ways in which schools use the evidence they have collected to set targets for improvement.

Setting and achieving targets for improving pupil progress and achievement

Our experience is that more and more schools are learning how to interpret the information they have collected in such a way as to be able to identify targets for improvement that directly concern pupils' learning, their progress and their achievement. To achieve these targets requires schools to pay close attention to any improvements needed in the quality of teaching in the classroom and to any implications for management arrangements beyond the classroom. This approach to school improvement is central to the new national guidelines on target setting (DfEE, 1997 forthcoming) which provide practical advice as to how schools can use the development planning process to enhance, much more directly, pupil progress and achievement.

We believe that a growing number of schools have learnt lessons about target setting from the experience of post-inspection action plans and from their own school improvement efforts. They have learnt that it is important to make the targets they set for pupils much more specific and explicit. They have learnt that it is also important, indeed essential, to identify at the outset how they will know they have made a difference. They are much clearer about the criteria and the evidence they will gather and use to evaluate the extent of their success in achieving the targets set.

In their guidance for schools on development planning, West Sussex LEA (1996) suggests that targets should be *SMART* as described in Table 5.4.

Table 5.3 described the procedures Portchester Secondary School (see page 87) uses to analyse and act upon mock GCSE results in order to set

Table 5.4   SMART targets

Specific (in relation to pupil achievement)

Measurable (in terms of pupil progress and achievement)

Achievable (within the resources of the school, including time and money)

Relevant (to the pupils and the school aims)

Time-related (within a realistic time-span and with an identified 'end date')

Source: West Sussex Education Department, 1996, p. 4.

targets for improvement. Once the results have been analysed by senior staff, a standard proforma is subsequently sent to each faculty requiring them to set faculty and pupil targets and to identify personal tutors for a small group of pupils. For each pupil their plans for the future in respect of examination targets are agreed and recorded in the pupil's National Record of Achievement. Staff who volunteer to work as a personal tutor to a designated individual or group of pupils are provided with the following clear brief:

> The purpose of the exercise is to work closely with a small group of pupils to encourage them to maximise their potential. It is suggested that you should see them at least once every fortnight, either individually or as a group.
> Some points to consider (in no particular order of importance):

- many researchers have suggested that pupils will make a greater effort because someone is taking a close interest in them (Hawthorne effect).
- identify whether the pupil wants to improve.
- identify what they want and where they want to be in nine months time.
- identify what they are prepared to do and how hard they are prepared to work in order to achieve their aims.
- help them to work out what changes they would need to make.
- discuss practical issues:
  e.g. Have they got a revision timetable? Are they keeping to it? How do they organise themselves for a session of revision? Perhaps they might wish to try and work with a partner or enlist the help of parents.
- set short-term achievable targets. 'I will work harder' is not good enough, but 'I will complete my maths coursework by Sunday night and show you on Monday' or 'On Tuesdays when I normally go out I will do two hours before going.'
- improve self-belief. Convince them that they can achieve their target, but only with a change of approach/attitude.
- encourage them to show you their National Record of Achievement. The information may be useful to you and confirm your interest in them.

Extract from Churchfield Primary School Development Plan

Detailed 1996/7 one year action plan
NAME OF PRIORITY: ART
Member of staff responsible for priority area:

A. BACKGROUND/Where are we now?
(Reference should be made to the evaluation outcomes, where available, on DP2)
The guidelines for ART skills have been devised to ensure progression. The common drawing task was repeated, providing a record of the children's skills and as an aid to teacher moderation.
Artists' work has been displayed around school, giving the children access to different types of painting, sculpture and design. Sketch books are being used effectively in KS2.
A lunchtime art club with an emphasis on 3D work was run for interested Year 6 pupils.
A professional artist worked with a group of Reception and Yr 6 children on a 6 week project based on photography. The children experimented with photography and simple photographic printing techniques. The project culminated in the making of a giant jigsaw puzzle.
Year 5 pupils visited the National Gallery.
Staff attended various art courses.
Reproduction posters of artists' work have been bought for art appreciation.

B. TARGETS/Where do we want to get to this year?
(Targets 1,2 3 etc) should be related to the implementation of the relevant policy statements where they are available)

Target No	Maintenance
1	To improve pupils' ability to extend their work and ensure progression; each classroom should be equipped with a variety of paints and drawing materials.
2	Improve the display of artwork, to value and promote art and enable the children to observe and evaluate their own and others' work.
	Development
3	Give children the opportunity to acquire a greater variety of skills and techniques through: (i) photography and simple darkroom printing techniques (ii) screen printing skills
4	Art club open to wider range

C. PLAN FOR IMPLEMENTATION, MANAGEMENT AND EVALUATION/How will we get there? *(Express as a series of tasks 1.1, 1.2 for target 1; 2.1, 2.2 for target 2, 3.1, 3.2 etc for target 3)*

Target No	Maintenance	When completed and person responsible
1	Order, distribute art materials – powder paint & containers, palettes, block/water colour paint, sketching pencils, pastels, charcoal and inks. School based inset for paint mixing skills	Sept 1996
2	Organise artifacts for easier access, improve storage, itemise resources & purchase	Aut 1996 S.K.
	Development	
3	Darkroom: (i) Find location, acquire equipment & materials. Run staff workshop on printing techniques (ii) Make screens. Run workshop for staff on screen printing techniques.	Aut 1996
4	Determine feasibility of art club for all age groups	Aut 1996 S. K.

Detailed 1996/7 one year action plan

D. PERFORMANCE INDICATORS (SUCCESS CRITERIA)/How will we know when we've got there?

(Performance indicators/success criteria should be agreed for each target)

Target No	Maintenance
1	Each classroom equipped with powder paints & containers, block or watercolour paints, palettes, sketching pencils, pastels, charcoal. Work reflecting the wide choice.
2	Quality work displayed. Children's art extended through observation and evaluation of the wider range of work displayed.
	Development
3	A list of resources will be available to staff.
	(i) Children using photography to record, experiment and broaden their ideas.
	(ii) Children using screen printing to extend their ideas and designs

E. STAFF DEVELOPMENT PLAN FOR PRIORITY AREA

(Match needs to the implementation tasks (1.1, 1.2, 2.1, 2.2 etc) Include details of activities, when done, by whom & staff involved)

Target No	Maintenance	Cost & Budget used school	other please specify
1	School based inset – to provide information and skills on painting techniques		
2	A session with each class during the summer term. Staff meeting with outside speaker on quality display (November)		
	Development		
3 (i)	Workshop to demonstrate to staff simple photographic printing techniques (October)		
(ii)	Workshop to demonstrate to staff at staff meetings screen printing techniques (September)		
	TOTAL INSET COSTS		

F. RESOURCE PLAN FOR PRIORITY AREA

(Match needs to the tasks (1.1, 1.2 etc) in the implementation plan)

Target No	Maintenance	Cost & Budget used school	other please specify
1	Art, craft & design materials (£1800)	1875	
2	Artifacts – artists' reproductions (£75)		
	Development		
3(i)	Equipment for darkroom – enlarger, tanks, safety light, chemicals	100	
(ii)	Screen mesh & material, screens	25	
	TOTAL RESOURCE COSTS		
	TOTAL OVERALL COST FOR PRIORITY	£2000	

Source: Churchfield Primary School

- the school will do all it can to help but in the end it's down to them.
- one of the most difficult parts may be a move towards behaving differently in front of their peers

STARTING POINTS

1. Predicted and target grades are in the Records of Achievement. Check through with them the number of predicted/targeted A-C grades.
2. Each pupil should have a revision programme. Get them to show it to you and explain how they intend using it.
3. Each pupil has a 'Learning Matters' booklet. Use this to reinforce good practice in revision techniques.

Among other things, Churchfield Primary School in north London identified art as a priority for improvement in their 1996/97 school development plan. The extract on pages 90–1 from the school's plan illustrates why the school identified the targets for improvement, what it intends to do – in other words, its action plan – and how it will know whether the improvements sought have been achieved.

In 1996 Enfield LEA launched a school improvement project. Schools were invited to submit a 'School-Based Project for Raising Achievement'. Chace Community School in Enfield took advantage of this initiative to improve the quality of their NRA process and below is an extract from the successful bid they made. It indicates the criteria by which the target group of pupils was selected and the procedures to be used to evaluate the outcomes.

The aim of the project is to improve the quality of the NRA process and enhance its status within the school community. The project will focus on individual student action-planning through academic tutoring and a mentoring scheme supported by adults other than teachers.

Pupils involved
NRA – Year 11 students
Academic tutoring – Year 11
Mentoring – 10 students selected by the following criteria: attendance – below 90% above 80%, punctuality – below 90%, coursework completion, academic performance, completion of homework.

Resources:
 Staffing
 –training of mentors
 –induction and training of Year 11 tutors in the process of NRA
 –evaluation workshop

 Inset
 –mentoring

 Materials/equipment
 –support and guidance materials related to the NRA

–package on academic tutoring
–travel expenses for mentors and students

Evaluation procedure (include any 'tests' to be used)
1. Predicted teacher assessments (TAs) in Year 11 – one to be completed in September, another in January.
2. Evaluating students' perceptions of the NRA – this will involve students in Year 12 to make a comparison.
3. Interview a randomised group of students to assess the quality of interaction between student and teacher in relation to achievement.

At the time of writing, the school is a few months into the project and the co-ordinator responsible for managing it described the progress made so far:

> The project has brought together in a coherent way a number of initiatives for raising achievement. The framework has enabled the school to establish stronger links between the academic and pastoral curriculum. The main vehicle for achieving the project aims is the development and implementation of a dynamic process for recording achievement through the National Record of Achievement (NRA). A number of milestones relating to the project have been achieved and are as follows:
> implementation of a training programme for all year 10 and 11 tutors and heads of faculty in student action planning;
> recruitment and training of mentors from the local business community;
> dissemination and consultation with parents and students securing support for the project;
> initial interview with students to identify targets has commenced;
> links have been established with the careers service to support the production of student action planning.

Often, target-setting involves targeting a particular group of pupils. Heavers Farm Primary School in south east London was concerned about the extent to which it was meeting the needs of more able pupils. However, the staff recognised they needed more evidence before they could set specific targets for this group of pupils. A brief for the special educational needs team was drawn up. It comprised the following questions.

THE MORE ABLE CHILD
SOME KEY QUESTIONS

- What can we learn from our individual experiences of teaching able or gifted children?
- Are the school's organisational measures adequate or should other strategies be developed?
- Is the school's monitoring and assessment process sufficiently refined to identify able and gifted pupils?
- Are there any barriers restricting the development of strategies felt appropriate for teaching able and gifted pupils? How might these be overcome?

- Should we be looking at a more coherent school-wide reward system? How might this work?
- Do we focus sufficiently on achievement or accept it with little comment?
- Do we recognise pupils with particular abilities? Is this information co-ordinated? Should a referral system be in place? How might it work?
- Do pupils have opportunities to work at a faster pace and to work independently?

As a result, the team then devised a staff questionnaire in which they provided guidance as to how to identify the more able pupil. By combining the information received from staff with other relevant evidence, the school was in a much better position to improve learning opportunities for this group of pupils.

Maintaining a focus on teaching and learning

The intelligent school understands that the quality of teaching and learning in the classroom must be the focus for improvement efforts and we have provided examples of the ways in which schools we know of have gone about this task. We have identified three main kinds of evidence that schools need to gather if they are to improve their effectiveness:

- entry data
- progress data
- comparative data.

From our experience more and more schools are recognising both the need and the importance of obtaining all three types of data. In this way, a school's improvement efforts relate directly to their own context and become rooted in and supported by *evidence* about pupils' learning in the classroom.

Hampstead Secondary School in north London, for example, has recognised this. Table 5.5 is a synopsis of the procedures the school uses to ensure that there is a sharp, rigorous focus on learning that involves the pupils, the staff, the governors and the parents in a structured partnership for improvement.

Similarly, Christ Church Primary School has recognised the importance of having effective planning procedures to improve the quality of teaching and learning in classrooms. It has also recognised the important 'feed forward' and 'feedback' role that assessment plays in the planning process. This has clear parallels with some of the characteristics of effective teaching explored in Chapter 3. It also relates to some of the intelligences we identify in the final chapter.

Table 5.5 Procedures for ensuring improvement

Focus on learning	Monitoring	Evaluation
Use of entry reading test scores	Use of student data base and issuing of data to teachers	Relating to attainment in lessons
Use of Entry numeracy test scores	Use of student data base and issuing of data to teachers	Relating to attainment in lessons
Use of cognitive thinking test scores (Kings Project)	Pilot study monitoring	Relate to other institutions and to future test results
Use of Primary Information including SATs results	Curriculum support, written report made available to staff	Review by curriculum support and Senior Executive
Departments developing portfolios of work at different levels following whole-staff agreement	Line management check on use	Development of an understanding of levels
Headteacher's analysis since 1984 of examination results and setting of annual targets – 94/95 to break 50% barrier of 5 A-C grades	Monitoring communicated to staff, students, parents and LEA	Development of ethos striving for improvement linked to strong emphasis on quality of teaching
Analysis of SATs results	Co-ordination by Examination and Assessment Co-ordinator and team of postholders	Comparisons by gender and ethnicity and across LEA
Analysis of GCSE results	Use of student data base and issuing of data to teachers	Relating to attainment in lessons
Analysis of A Level results	Use of student data base and issuing of data to teachers	Relating to attainment in lessons
Team on Assessment and Differentiation development of whole-school policy on assessment and marking	Analysis of departmental practice across the school	Development of whole-school approaches
Use of whole staff inset to develop awareness, whole-school policies.	Whole-staff analysis of current practice and sharing of best practice	Development of reflective practice
School Development Plan major target since September 94	Monitoring by Senior Executive	Evaluation of SDP targets and setting of new developmental targets for the next SDP
LEA/NFER value-added monitoring of SATs and GCSE results	Report on 1995 results	Use to target areas of weakness with line managers
Examination and Assessment Co-ordinator analysis of results and comparison with national norms	Analysis shown graphically to emphasise strengths and weaknesses	Line management with HODs and HOY to focus on areas below the national average and to set targets
Student Work Reviews with Senior Staff/Tutors/Other Staff/Governors	Monitoring, student planners, all written books and student self-assessment	Identification of inconsistencies, difficulties which can be followed up by Head/Senior Executive team. This may lead to support and pressure followed by target setting.
Whole-staff inset briefing on value-added ALIS and YELIS	Establishing responsibility for value-added on Senior Teacher job description	
Uses of Ofsted materials for inset with staff	Means of moving towards consistency	Ofsted report and action plan
League Tables	Analysis	To establish position relative to other comparable schools

Source: Hampstead Secondary School

As a result of having this understanding, the school has brought together in one document a policy on 'Planning, Assessment and Record-Keeping' which, like Hampstead, involves all the stakeholders. The policy, which is in a loose-leaf binder format and so can be added to and amended easily, is more like a scheme of work. As well as spelling out principles it also spells out how the policy works in practice. All the way through the pupils' progress and achievements are the cornerstone of the document. The 'policy in action' is underpinned by a shared agreement amongst all the staff about classroom organisation, about how to respond to and mark pupils' work and about how to deal with any behavioural problems including bullying. What follows is a description of the policy and then extracts from it in the order in which they are numbered in the text are provided at the end of the chapter.

The policy begins with an affirmation of the key principles of learning (1). The school reviews these annually to ensure they continue to underpin other policy reviews and inform classroom practice. The key principles of planning are then set out (2). These are followed by a description of the detailed, practical ways in which pupils' work is to be planned. Three levels of curriculum planning are identified (3). Each of these is defined and then supported by practical, standard planning formats. Other types of planning such as planning for positive behaviour are also included.

Assessment and record-keeping are dealt with in a similar way using a combination of 'home-grown' procedures and systems developed by the local authority. The principles of assessment and record-keeping were described earlier (see pages 77).

The final section of the document concerns practical strategies for implementing priorities for improvement and monitoring the extent to which the planning, record-keeping and assessment policy is contributing to improvements in teaching and learning in the classroom. There is a common pro-forma for an individual action plan which each member of staff has to complete to show how they intend to implement any priorities in the school development plan for which they have responsibility. The format enables staff to identify the target(s) for improvement, what needs to be done, when, by whom and how much it will cost in time, money, people and materials and the implications for staff development. Staff record how the action to be taken is to be monitored and the evidence to be gathered in relation to a set of outcomes the teacher expects to achieve.

Systems to enable the headteacher and deputy head to observe and monitor the quality of teaching and learning in classrooms are also incorporated in the document. These include a management plan for improving teaching and learning (4), a set of criteria developed by the staff for assessing the quality of learning and teaching (5) and a format for monitoring standards of achievement (6). The document concludes with a copy of the Annual Report that is sent out to every parent the format of which was developed by the local authority.

It is hardly surprising that when inspected by Ofsted this 'policy in action' received high praise not least because it was seen to work in practice for teachers and pupils in the classroom. Inspectors (Inspection Report No. 100489, 1996, pp. 11–12) reported that:

> The school has a very comprehensive policy for Planning, Assessment and Record-Keeping. This provides the framework for planning learning and recording progress which contributes substantially to the good standards of teaching and learning achieved within the school.

This is surely the acid test of any policy concerned to bring about improvements in teaching and learning. The way this school has managed to *put the pieces together* in relation to these three key aspects of teaching and learning has all the hallmarks of *the intelligent school*.

Conclusion

The intelligent school knows that improving the quality of teaching and learning in the classroom must be the cornerstone of its improvement efforts. This chapter has provided practical examples of how schools can go about this task. The focus has been on ways of finding out about pupils' progress and achievement in order to make *intelligent* decisions about what pupils need to learn next.

The intelligent school also knows that classrooms are not islands. The work that goes on in them needs to be co-ordinated across the school as a whole if pupils' progress and achievement are to be sustained and enhanced further. In the final chapter we consider the implications of this for the school as a whole.

Questions for discussion

1. Are your school's improvement efforts sufficiently focused on pupils' progress and achievement? How do you involve pupils in this process?

2. How do you find out about:

   (a) what your pupils know and can do when they first come to you?

   (b) how much progress they are making from year to year?

   (c) whether their levels of achievement are good enough by your standards and by local and national standards?

3. How effective are you at setting and implementing targets to improve pupil progress and achievement? What lessons have you learnt?

4. Which aspects of teaching and learning in the classroom are a particular strength in the school and which aspects need further improvement?

Christ Church Primary School
THE SCHOOL'S STATEMENT OF KEY PRINCIPLES OF CHILDREN'S LEARNING

Our aim is for the full development of the personality and abilities of each child so that s/he learns to be independent, self-motivated, to possess a sense of self-respect and to respect others.

In order to achieve these aims:

The children need to acquire knowledge, skills and practical abilities, and to be instilled with a desire to use them;
They need to develop qualities of mind, spirit, feeling and imagination;
They need to appreciate human achievements and aspirations;
They need to acquire a set of ethical values and moral standards by which to live, respect other races, religions and ways of life and to begin to understand the world in which they live and the interdependence of groups and nations.

We aim to encourage each child:

to read with enjoyment fluently and accurately with understanding, feeling and discrimination.
to develop a legible style of handwriting and high standard of spelling, syntax, punctuation and usage.
to communicate clearly and confidently in speech and writing in ways appropriate to various occasions and purposes.
to listen and respond appropriately.
to learn how to acquire information from various sources and to record information and findings in a variety of ways, including Information Technology.
to understand the application of mathematical ideas in various situations in home, school and local area.
to apply computational skills with speed and accuracy.
to observe and develop curiosity about living and inanimate things, to respect them and to recognise characteristics such as pattern and order.
to explore basic scientific ideas and to investigate solutions and interpret evidence, to analyse and solve problems.
to know and understand the geographical, historical and social aspects of the local environment and the national heritage and to recognise the multi-cultural nature of the world in which we live.
to use and control their bodies in physical activities and to develop the finer control necessary for manipulative skills.
to develop the desire and the skills necessary to express themselves through the creative arts, dance, drama, music, art, design/technology.
to develop awareness of self and sensitivity to others, to develop patterns of self-discipline and acceptable behaviour in order to acquire a set of moral values and the confidence to hold moral judgements.

KEY PRINCIPLES OF PLANNING

There needs to be consistency and quality in our approach to planning. These principles will inform the way we plan and should be reviewed regularly.

Planning should:

start from where the children are and build on their identified knowledge, skills and concepts to ensure progression and continuity in their learning.

be based on clear information about the child's achievement through assessment and records.

be clear, concise and focused: i.e. showing what is being taught, how the children will learn, and what they will do.

take account of time in order to ensure balance, breadth and depth.

be realistic within given timescales.

include all core areas of the National Curriculum, the Foundation Subjects, as well as Religious Education and P.H.S.E., and indicate the Programmes of Study to be covered.

make purposeful and meaningful connections between the different areas of the curriculum.

take account of equal opportunities issues re: grouping of children, resourcing and subject matter.

be provided for SEN pupils.

show how learning will be differentiated to meet a range of needs.

be available for parents, teachers, governors, senior staff and inspectors.

be clearly explained to children in the course of the teaching process.

be evaluated to assess its effectiveness.

it should be: MANAGEABLE   REALISTIC   DIFFERENTIATED

3.   THE THREE LEVELS OF CURRICULUM PLANNING

LONG TERM

CURRICULUM MAP

Each year group has a curriculum map which covers all National Curriculum Subjects and Religious Education. It states the broad areas to be studied during the term or half term.

POLICY

Each subject should have a policy which ensures consistency of approach and delivery across the school.

SCHEMES OF WORK

Each subject should have a scheme of work which gives detailed guidance on what is to be taught and suggestions on how it can be achieved.

TERMLY PLAN

This outlines skills and knowledge to be covered during the term in each subject.

MEDIUM TERM

HALF TERMLY PLAN

This should show how the curriculum is organised over a half term in order to cover the Programmes of Study in each area. Where appropriate the element of the Programme of Study being taught should be stated.

HALF TERMLY REVIEW

This ensures that the outcomes of planning are evaluated and planning moves forward as a result of this. (Did you teach what you planned to teach? What did the children achieve?)

INDIVIDUAL EDUCATION PLAN

Each child on the SEN register has an I.E.P. with clear, specific and achievable targets. They are reviewed systematically and used as working documents.

SHORT TERM

WEEKLY PLANS

These should include teaching aims and the learning experience for the children, referring to the specific element of the programmes of study. Weekly planning should show progression and consolidation within the aims and learning experiences.

SPECIAL PLANS

I.E.P.s are broken down on a weekly basis (where appropriate), so that we know:
    when a target is being addressed
    how this is being done
    who is doing this
These are handed in weekly with curriculum plans and are an important communication tool.

4. HEAD/DEPUTY MONITORING

CHRIST CHURCH CE PRIMARY SCHOOL
MANAGEMENT PLAN FOR IMPROVING TEACHING & LEARNING
Classroom Visits (Head and Deputy)

Date Start Time	R	1	2	3	4	5	6
Was the teacher teaching/ supporting?							
All children on task?							
If on task do they understand task? subject?							
Our opinion of books/ presentation?							
Start/end lesson?							
Overall impression of environment?							
General comments – whole school?							

5. CLASSROOM OBSERVATIONS

Quality of Learning	Quality of Teaching
Behaviour aids learning Range of learning opportunities in tasks set Perseverance/keeping to task Children motivated Selection of appropriate methods Selection of appropriate resources Confidence in the tasks Pupils clear Enthusiasm and understanding to discuss work Co-operation/Collaboration Applying knowledge	Planning Interaction with children Quality of questioning Quality of exposition Expectations Match of work to ability of children Management of the learning Pace appropriate Match of method suited to lesson and materials Good relationships teacher to children, children to children, children to teacher Differentiation, achievable targets Supportive intervention Evaluative intervention

6. MONITORING ACHIEVEMENT			
CLASS/YEAR:	**TEACHER:**	**SUBJECT:**	**KS:**

Pre-Experience & Attainment		
	TA	SATs

Planning/Activities/Tasks (incl. Consolidation & Extension:)		
	ATs	LEVELS

Marking/Comments

Planning Related to Outcomes

1 Very good	4 Unsatisfactory
2 Good	5 Poor
3 Satisfactory	

General Comments

REF:	TAs	Ind. Ass. Folders	ATs

HEAD/DEPUTY MONITORING

Source: Christ Church Primary School

6

The intelligent school – putting the pieces together

Today's problems come from yesterday's solutions.

(Senge, 1993, p. 57)

Schools serve the needs of the present and the future. They have a crucial role to play in the lives and learning of their pupils now and as they inherit the daunting and exciting tasks that face them as citizens in the twenty-first century. They also have a responsibility for future students. Roland Barth (1988) has described a school as 'four walls surrounding the future'.

Michael Barber (1996, p. 17) comments on the particular challenges awaiting young people in school now:

> Of course in the past there were scourges of disease, famine and conflict, but until recently these were often considered beyond the powers of human solution: they were acts of God. No one until the mid-twentieth century believed, or even pretended, that mankind had the power to shape its destiny, or to destroy it. This generation and its successors cannot pass the buck. It is their destiny to inherit a unique combination of unparalleled power and terrible responsibility.

This concluding chapter concerns the school as a whole. It draws the themes from the previous chapters together in order to paint a portrait of *the intelligent school* which conveys the wholeness of the enterprise in which schools are engaged. The picture that emerges provides a new way of looking at schools as organisations that reflects both their dynamic and their organic nature. Inspired by Gardner's (1983) work on multiple intelligence we use the idea of *intelligence* to convey a new image. We portray a very different picture from some previous, more mechanistic images of schools. Our task is not so much to challenge existing school improvement efforts as to suggest that we may need to bring some fresh thought to bear on their purpose and process.

Nine intelligences for successful schools

We have observed *nine intelligences* in successful schools, although, as with Gardner's seven intelligences, we are not suggesting that they are finite as there may well be others. The nine are listed in Table 6.1.

Table 6.1 Nine intelligences

1. Contextual intelligence

2. Strategic intelligence

3. Academic intelligence

4. Reflective intelligence

5. Pedagogical intelligence

6. Collegial intelligence

7. Emotional intelligence

8. Spiritual intelligence

9. Ethical intelligence

These nine intelligences seem to us to be used by a school in the process of addressing simultaneously the core business of learning, teaching, effectiveness and improvement. They enable schools to *put the pieces together*. In other words, they are used to combine the different 'threads' running through the previous five chapters. The way in which we are using the term 'intelligence' is not straightforward because it is not easily observable and is even harder to measure. It is a range of collective capacities schools have that enable them to achieve their goals successfully. It involves the use of wisdom, insight, intuition and experience as well as knowledge, skills and understanding. These intelligences provide something analogous to the fuel, water, and oil in a car. They all have discrete functions but, for their success, need to work together.

1. *Contextual intelligence*

Contextual intelligence is the capacity of a school to see itself in relationship to its wider community and the world of which it is a part. It is characterised by a welcoming responsiveness to visitors, new ideas and events in the immediate environment. It is also characterised by a self-organising capacity. This is *not* the same as being autonomous. It is the capacity we have tried to describe which a school needs to match its decisions and direction to its context.

Intelligent schools have a capacity to 'read their overall context' in a way that they are neither overwhelmed by it nor distanced from it but are in a healthy relationship with it and know they need to respond to both its positive and negative aspects. Self-organisation refers to *the intelligent school*'s ability to respond, think and act in ways that meet the varied requirements of its context both external and internal. It is also characterised by a school's capacity to be flexible and to work openly with a range of perspectives, listening to others, particularly in the local community, whilst not losing sight of its core purpose and aims.

Intelligent schools understand the key messages, described in Chapter 1, that have emerged from school improvement studies. For example, they know there are no blueprints or quick fixes because they, whilst like every other school in many ways, are unique and so they are not overly dependent on solutions to come from outside and are developing problem-solving strategies themselves. At the same time, they are aware of and sensitive to the need to work in collaboration, not competition, with other schools so as to learn with and from them.

Self-organisation is a term originally borrowed from the study of living systems and Margaret Wheatley (1992, p. 91) in her writing has been applying some of what we know from ecology about the functioning of the natural world to the workings of human organisations. She also refers to the capacity of the 'self-organising' organisation to renew itself:

> We are beginning to see organisations that tap into this property of self-organising or self-renewing systems . . . . Both types of organisation avoid rigid or permanent structures and instead develop a capacity to respond to a need. When the need changes, so does the organisational structure.

In the context of exploring features of self-renewing systems, Garmston and Wellman (1995, p. 8) suggest that:

> if adaptivity is the central operating principle for successful organisations and for successful schools, then we must search for sources of energy to vitalise this process.

2. *Strategic intelligence*

Strategic intelligence includes the finding from the effectiveness literature that clarity about goals is essential and that the aims and purposes of the school need to be shared by everyone. *The intelligent school* is able to bring together in a strategic way the core and related characteristics of effectiveness illustrated in Figure 1.1 on page 7. It is able to plan the action needed to achieve improvement and has the capacity to put vision into practice. This capacity involves the ability to establish the corporate type of development plan described in Chapter 1 – a plan in which the long-term priorities for improvement are kept under regular review and revised in the light of new contextual information. It is the kind of plan that is evolutionary (Louis and Miles, 1992) in nature. Hence the school has an approach to planning that enables it to anticipate and manage change. Hopewell (1996, p. 903) reviewing Michael McMaster's (1995) book states that:

> In a fast changing environment this (the traditional approach) may not respond quickly enough. An uncertain future may make our current strategy a threat to longevity . . . . We need a strategy concerned with creating the future, not merely with adapting to one that is happening already.

Strategic intelligence is about responding appropriately to the present, creating the future and anticipating the consequences.

3. *Academic intelligence*

Academic intelligence concerns the value put on high quality study and scholarship. We have referred to this intelligence throughout the book particularly in relation to the concept of value-added, the characteristics of effective learning and teaching and the key importance of high expectations. This type of intelligence is distinguished by an ethos that actively encourages pupils' engagement in their learning. This intelligence values pupils' questions, contributions and search for meaning. It is prepared to teach and coach pupils in the processes of enquiry and encourages high achievement and performance.

Some of the ways in which schools put this academic intelligence into practice were described in Chapter 5. A common feature of the examples is a sense that the pupils really matter. Maybe this is stating the obvious but it is not always obvious to pupils.

Academic intelligence also values and promotes teachers' learning because it recognises that it is inextricably linked with pupils' learning. This was a key theme in Chapter 4 which was developed further in Chapter 5. Academic intelligence also encourages efficacy for both staff and pupils.

> To be efficacious is to believe one can achieve, and to be willing to exert the effort necessary to achieve. Efficacious people have an almost unassailable belief in the likelihood of their own success, work harder than those that are not efficacious, persevere through failures and disappointments, and experience less stress.
>
> (Garmston and Wellman, 1995, p. 9)

This is what we described as the '*can do*' factor in Chapter 2.

4. *Reflective intelligence*

Reflective intelligence covers the core skills and processes of monitoring, reflecting upon and evaluating the effectiveness of the school in general and, in particular, the progress and achievement of the pupils which was the key theme in Chapter 5. Reflecting upon the progress and achievement of pupils is a central concern and as such it is closely interrelated with academic intelligence. This is because integral to this reflective capacity is an awareness of the dangers of low expectations for pupils on the one hand and complacency, for example, about their seemingly good examination results on the other.

Through collecting, analysing, interpreting and using a range of information the school can judge effectiveness by drawing on its contextual intelligence and plan improvements by drawing on its strategic intelligence. The data used to reflect upon the pupils' learning includes, not just statistical information and other data collected formally, but the harder to evaluate formative data that necessitates evidence to change an assumption or prejudice into a properly substantiated judgement. *The intelligent school* is comfortable and skilled in its ability to interpret and use information and put it to the service of its pupils and the organisation as a whole. The school knows how to learn from the data and what the data mean as many of the examples in Chapter 5 illustrated.

5. *Pedagogical intelligence*

Pedagogical intelligence was largely outlined in Chapters 2, 3 and 4. It is characterised by the school seeing itself as a learning organisation: learning about learning. It has a commitment to study and deepen its understanding about its core purpose. Pedagogical intelligence ensures that learning and teaching are regularly being examined and developed: they are never an orthodoxy that remains unexamined.

This dimension of intelligence recognises the dynamic relationship between learning and teaching which was described in Chapters 2 and 3 and understands the notion of 'fitness for purpose' that was developed in these chapters. It also understands the dynamic relationship between thinking, learning and teaching and that the process of metacognition, defined in Chapter 2, is an essential aspect of *the intelligent school*.

A recent publication commissioned by the National Union of Teachers (NUT/University of Strathclyde, 1995, p. 9) states that:

> In teaching, as in many professions, the commitment to critical systematic reflection on practice as a basis for individual and collective development is at the heart of what it means to be a professional.

6. *Collegial intelligence*

Collegial intelligence describes the capacity for staff in particular to work together to improve their practice in the classroom. The key theme in Chapter 4 was that *the intelligent school* understands the need to support teachers' learning continuously in a variety of ways.

Underpinning collegial intelligence is a recognition that whilst individuals can make a difference, the sum of the parts is greater than the whole when staff work together to improve and develop one another's practice. Collegial intelligence stems from an understanding of the relationship between teachers' learning and school improvement and concerns the capacity, described in Chapter 1, to enable teachers to be the main agents of change. The benefits to the school as a whole of this aspect of intelligence were described in Chapter 4 and articulated by Roland Barth (1990) (see page 59).

7. *Emotional intelligence*

Emotional intelligence is to do with a school's capacity to allow the feelings of both pupils and staff to be owned, expressed and respected. As we described in Chapter 2, Howard Gardner (1983) distinguishes between interpersonal and intrapersonal intelligence.

Interpersonal intelligence is the ability to understand other people: what motivates them, how to work co-operatively with them. Intrapersonal intelligence is a correlative ability turned inward. It is the capacity to form an accurate model of oneself and to be able to use that model to operate effectively in life.

Goleman (1996, p. 34) argues that emotional intelligence is a vital capacity for learning. It includes motivation, persistence, control of impulse, regulation of mood and keeping distress from swamping the ability to think. In many respects it is an essential part of the pact between the teacher and the learner which was a key theme developed in Chapter 2.

Salovey and Mayer (1990) have summarised five aspects of emotional intelligence: self-awareness; managing emotions; motivating oneself; recognising emotions in others; and handling relationships. All these aspects impinge on the teaching and learning process which illustrates their close connection with academic intelligence.

8. *Spiritual intelligence*

The national inspection Framework (Education (Schools) Act 1992) has, for the first time, required schools to demonstrate how they plan to ensure the spirituality of their pupils is fostered. Because of its essentially ephemeral nature this has resulted in much interest and discussion as to how this should be done. A *Handbook* (1995) produced as part of a recent project on *Values and Visions* (Burns and Lamont, 1995, p. xiii) states that:

> Spirituality is a source of creativity open to us all. It brings that quality of aliveness which sparks inquiry, ideas, observations, insights, empathy, artistic expression, earnest endeavour and playfulness. It opens us to life and to each other. Spirituality is a thread that runs through our life, bringing hope, compassion, thankfulness, courage, peace and a sense of purpose and meaning to the everyday, while reaching beyond the immediate world of the visible and tangible. It drives us to seek and stay true to values not ruled by material success.

Each school will define spirituality differently but, for the purposes of this book, spiritual intelligence is characterised by a fundamental valuing of the lives and development of all members of a school community: that they all matter and have something to contribute. It also recognises the need to balance the busy life of a school community with times of peace and an opportunity to be in touch with ultimate issues. It values that in our experience which is neither tangible nor measurable. It also concerns the capacity, as described in Chapter 2, to enable deep learning to occur.

9.   *Ethical intelligence*

A theme throughout the book has been that *the intelligent school* recognises the importance of pupils' rights and the need to involve pupils in decisions about their own learning. Ethical intelligence incorporates the clear statement of values and beliefs covered in a school's aims statement. It concerns the way a school conveys its moral purpose and principles such as justice and equity. It is characterised by a concern to ensure access for all pupils to a broad and balanced curriculum and a concern about the distribution and use of resources. The concept of entitlement is seen as important with the result that support for learning is highly valued and there is an understanding about the nature of learners and what learners want as described in Chapter 2.

Such schools recognise that they have a long-term responsibility to future pupils in the community as well as an immediate responsibility to those pupils currently attending the school.

Our encounters with schools that have an ethical intelligence suggest that they have high self-esteem as an organisation which is not the same as complacency. They rarely feel totally satisfied about what they are doing. They usually have ideas about how they can do even better next time. Sara Lawrence Lightfoot (1983, p. 310) found that:

> This more modest orientation towards goodness does not rest on absolute or discrete qualities of excellence and perfection, but on views of institutions that anticipate change, conflict and imperfection.

Conclusion

Our original intention when planning this book was to argue that knowledge about the combined characteristics of effective:

- schools
- improvement efforts
- learning, and
- teaching

would strengthen a school's capacity to raise standards and enhance pupils' progress and achievement. We know now that this knowledge is still not enough in itself. All important is what a school does with the knowledge; *how* it uses it to improve its own effectiveness. What marks out *the intelligent school* is its ability to apply the knowledge and skills it has to maximum effect in classrooms and across the school as a whole. We would argue, from what we have read and from our personal experience, that it does this through the combined use of the nine intelligences we have identified. There is an understanding that these multiple intelligences are interdependent.

Interdependence is an underlying theme in the recent literature about organisations. Michael McMaster (1995) suggests that, as a species, we are still bound up in a world view that is mechanistic, reductionist and essentially rational. Many writers, particularly in the fields of organisational transformation and the new sciences (Wheatley, 1992; Senge, 1993; Capra, 1996) suggest that the views that have been held of how the world works since Descartes and Newton are changing. This is referred to variously as the post-modern view, post-industrialism, the age of information, the ecological paradigm. What these writers suggest is that a renewed sense and understanding of the interconnections of all life is developing and that the now well-known phrase 'the whole is greater than the sum of its parts' is more true than perhaps the glib way the phrase is used tends to suggest. The term 'organisation' is seen to refer to 'the pattern of connections between parts' (McMaster, 1995, p. 7). A classic example of this concept is the interdependence between teaching and support staff within a school. Both groups have different roles to play but, to maximise their effectiveness, each depends on the other.

Also writing on this theme, David Bohm (1980, p. 1) suggests an urgency to working with this understanding:

> for fragmentation is now very widespread, not only through society, but in each individual; and this is leading to a kind of general confusion of the mind, which creates a series of problems and interferes with our clarity of perception so seriously as to prevent us from being able to solve most of them . . . . The notion that all these fragments are separately existent is

evidently an illusion, and this illusion cannot do other than lead to endless conflict and confusion.

Those researching in this field are also reinforcing the nature of flux and change at the heart of reality and that 'this means that our understanding is ever changing based on continued inquiry, exploration and dialogue' (McMaster, 1995, p. 4). This resonates with some of the characteristics of *the intelligent school* we have identified in this book. McMaster (1995, p. 3) develops this theme of the relationship between the parts and the whole by using the term *corporate intelligence*. He writes that:

> the possibility of a corporate intelligence . . . is that more information, more richness of interpretation, more creativity in processing information, and more generative ability can be integrated beyond what any single individual can do.

This applies as much to human service organisations like schools as to business and commercial organisations. In many respects the corporate style of school development planning (MacGilchrist *et al.*, 1995) we described in Chapter 1 reflects the understanding and values we are suggesting are at the heart of *the intelligent school*. Table 6.2 summarises the characteristics of the corporate intelligence of *the intelligent school*.

Putting the pieces together of school effectiveness and improvement with teaching and learning then is not a mechanistic or linear activity. It involves a capacity to think and act in ways that simultaneously enable what we have referred to in Chapter 5 as the classroom exceeding and the classroom perceiving perspectives to come together and be integrated with a school exceeding perspective. In other words, a capacity to work at the interdependence between the school and the classroom and the school and its community in such a way that the whole is greater than the sum of the parts.

In his introduction to 'The Fifth Discipline' Peter Senge (1993, p. 4) explores this theme:

> From a very early age, we are taught to break apart problems, to fragment the world. This apparently makes complex tasks and subjects more manageable, but we pay a hidden, enormous price. We can no longer see the consequences of our actions; we lose our intrinsic sense of connection to a larger whole. When we then try to see 'the big picture' we try to reassemble the fragments in our minds, to list and organise all the pieces. But as physicist David Bohm says (part of this quote), the task is futile – similar to trying to reassemble the fragments of a broken mirror to see a true reflection. Thus after a while we give up trying to see the whole altogether. The tools and ideas presented in this book are for destroying the illusion that the world is created of separate, unrelated forces. When we give up this illusion – we can then build 'learning organisations', organisations where people can continually expand their capacity to create the results

Table 6.2   The Corporate Intelligence of the Intelligent School

1.	Contextual intelligence	– understands the relationship between the school and the wider community – able to read internal and external context – flexible and adaptable – knows 'no quick fixes'
2.	Strategic intelligence	– uses contextual intelligence to establish clear goals – establishes shared aims and purposes – puts vision into practice through planned improvements
3.	Academic intelligence	– emphasises achievement and scholarship – values pupils' engagement in and contribution to learning – values and promotes teachers' learning – encourages the 'can do' factor
4.	Reflective intelligence	– monitors and evaluates the work of the school – uses data to judge effectiveness and plan improvement – uses data to reflect, in particular, on pupils' progress and achievement
5.	Pedagogical intelligence	– emphasises learning about pupils' learning – ensures learning and teaching are regularly examined and developed – challenges orthodoxies
6.	Collegial intelligence	– views the staff as learners – improves practice in the classroom through teachers working together
7.	Emotional intelligence	– values expression of feelings – understands others and how to work co-operatively – individuals understand themselves – encourages motivation, persistence and understands failure
8.	Spiritual intelligence	– has compassion – values the development and contribution of all members of the school and its community – creates space to reflect on ultimate issues
9.	Ethical intelligence	– has clear values and beliefs – has a sense of moral purpose and principle – is committed to access and entitlement for all – has high but not complacent self-esteem

they truly desire, where new and expansive patterns of thinking are nurtured, where collective aspiration is set free, and where people are continually learning how to learn together.

This view of a school as an organisation is a different one from images of the school as a loose federation of different classrooms in which the teacher is predominantly autonomous and unaccountable to the whole; a classroom similar to the one in which many of us would have started teaching. 'Sink or swim' was the order of the day. Expectations were that once you had learnt to teach, you certainly should not need to keep learning, unless there was something wrong with you.

Our view is that by broadening our collective understanding of the range of intelligences that schools are already using and have the potential to develop, more energy will be released to adapt swiftly to the needs not only of the present but also of the future. Intelligence, in this sense, describes what is already happening as well as what can be learnt and improved upon. Used in this way it is an empowering notion – empowering for us and for the lives and learning of our pupils now and in the future.

Bibliography

Abbott, J. (1994) Learning Makes Sense: Re-creating Education for a Changing Future, *Education 2000*, Letchworth.

Alexander, R., Rose, J. and Woodhead, C. (1992) *Curriculum Organisation and Classroom Practice in Primary Schools – A Discussion Paper*, HMSO, London.

Armstrong, T. (1994) *Multiple Intelligences in the Classroom*, ASCD, Alexandria, Va.

Aspy, D. and Roebuck, F. (1976) *A Lever Long Enough*, National Consortium for Humanizing Education (PO Box 1001), Washington DC.

Barber, M. (1993) Great Expectations, *Education*, 30 July.

Barber, M. (1996) *The Learning Game: Arguments for an Education Revolution*, Victor Gollancz, London.

Barth, R. (1988) Vision and School Improvement, in *Improving Schools for the Twenty-First Century* F. W. Parkay, (ed), Univ. of Florida.

Barth, R. (1990) *Improving Schools from Within*, Jossey-Bass, San Francisco, CA.

Belenky, M., Clinchy, B., Goldberger, N. R. and Tarule, J. M. (1986) *Women's Way of Knowing. The Development of Self, Voice and Mind*, Basic Books, New York

Bennett, N., Desforges, C., Cockburn, A. and Wilkinson, B. (1984) *The Quality of Pupil Learning Experiences*, Lawrence Erlbaum Associates, London.

Bennis, W. and Nanus, B. (1985) *Leaders*, Harper & Row, New York.

Beresford, J. (1995) *Classroom Conditions for School Improvement: A Literature Review*, Institute of Education, University of Cambridge (mimeo).

Block, P. (1987) *The Empowered Manager*, Jossey-Bass, San Francisco, CA.

Bohm, D. (1980) *Wholeness and the Implicate Order*, Routledge and Kegan Paul, London.

Bolam, R., McMahon, A., Pocklington, K. and Weindling, D. (1993) *Effective Management in Schools*, HMSO, London.

Bruner, J. S. (1960) *The Process of Education*, Harvard University Press, Massachusetts.

Bruner, J. S. (1996) *The Culture of Education*, Harvard University Press, London, England.

Burns, S. and Lamont, G. (1995) *Values and Visions, Handbook for Spiritual Development and Global Awareness*, Hodder & Stoughton.

Capra, F. (1996) *The Web of Life*, Harper Collins, London.

Chrispeels, J. (1992) *Purposeful Restructuring: Creating a Culture for Learning and Achievement in Elementary Schools*, Falmer Press, Lewes.

Cooper, P. and McIntyre, D. (1996) The Importance of Power-Sharing in Class-room Learning, in M. Hughes (ed) *Teaching and Learning in Changing Times*, Blackwell, Oxford.

Cuban, L. (1988) Why Do Some Reforms Persist? *Educational Administration Quarterly*, Vol. 24, no. 3, pp. 329–35.

Daniels, H., Hey, V., Leonard, D. and Smith, M. (1996) *Gender and Special Needs Provision in Mainstream Schooling*, ESRC Report no. R000235059.

Deal, T. E. (1987) The culture of schools, in L. T. Sheive and M. B. Schoenheit (eds) *Leadership: Examining the Elusive, 1987 Yearbook of the Association for Supervision and Curriculum Development*, ASCA, Arlington, Va.

DFE (1994) *Raising Standards of Achievement in Education: Lessons from the GEST Experience*, The Planning Exchange, Manchester.

DFE/Ofsted (1995) *Governing Bodies and Effective Schools*, DFE, London.

DfEE (1997 forthcoming) *New Guidance on Target Setting*, DfEE, London.

Dryden, G. and Vos, J. (1994) *The Learning Revolution*, Accelerated Learning, Aylesbury, Bucks.

Edmonds, R. R. (1979) Some Schools Work and More Can, *Social Policy*, Vol. 9, p. 28–32.

Education Counts (1991) Special Study Panel on Education Indicators, Washington DC.

Education (Schools) Act (1992) Section 9.

Eisner, E. (1985) *The Art of Educational Evaluation*, Falmer Press, Lewes.

Entwistle, N. J. and Entwistle, A. C. (1991) Forms of Understanding for Degree Examinations: the Pupil Experience and its Implications, *Higher Education*, Vol. 22, pp. 205–27.

Feden, P. D. (1994) About Instruction: Powerful New Strategies Worth Knowing, *Educational Horizons*, pp. 18–24.

Fennema, E. (1983) Success in Mathematics, in M. Marland (ed), *Sex Differentiation and Schooling*, Heinemann Educational Books, London.

Fink, D. and Stoll, L. (in press) Linking School and Teacher Development, in T. Townsend (ed) *Restructuring and Quality in Tomorrow's Schools*, Routledge, London.

Fullan, M. G. (1991) *The New Meaning of Educational Change*, Cassell, London.

Fullan, M. G. (1992) *What's Worth Fighting for in Headship*, Open University Press, Milton Keynes.

Fullan, M. G., Bennett, B. and Rolheiser-Bennett, C. (1990) Linking Classroom and School Improvement, *Educational Leadership*, Vol. 47, no. 8, pp. 13–19.

Fullan, M. and Hargreaves, A. (1994) The Teacher as a Person, in A. Pollard, and J. Bourne (eds) *Teaching and Learning in the Primary School*, Routledge, London.

Galton, M. (1980) *Progress and Performance in the Primary Classroom*, Routledge and Kegan Paul, London.

Galton, M. (1989) *Teaching in the Primary School*, David Fulton, London.

Gardner, H. (1983) *Frames of Mind: the Theory of Multiple Intelligences*, Basic Books, New York.

Gardner, H. (1993a) *Multiple Intelligences: The Theory in Practice*, Basic Books, New York.

Gardner, H. (1993b) *The Unschooled Mind*, Fontana Press, London.

Garmston, R. and Wellman, B. (1995) Adaptive Schools in a Quantum Universe, *Educational Leadership*, Vol. 52, no. 7, pp. 6–12.

Gillborn, D. and Gipps, C. (1996) *Recent Research on the Achievements of Ethnic Minority Pupils*, Ofsted.

Gilligan, C. (1982) *In a Different Voice*, Harvard University Press, Cambridge, Mass.

Gipps, C. (1992) What We Know About Effective Primary Teaching, *The London File*, Tufnell Press, London.

Gipps, C. (1994) *Beyond Testing: Towards a Theory of Educational Assessment*, Falmer Press, London.

Gipps, C., and Murphy, P. (1994) *A Fair Test? Assessment, Achievement and Equity*, Open University Press, Milton Keynes.

Goleman, D. (1996) *Emotional Intelligence: Why it Matters More than IQ*, Bloomsbury Paperbacks, London.

Goldstein, H. (1996) Relegate the Leagues, in *New Economy*, The Dryden Press, pp. 199–203.

Goldstein, H. and Spiegelhalter, D. (1996) League Tables and their Limitations: Statistical Issues in Comparisons of Institutional Importance, *Journal of the Royal Statistical Society*, pp. 385–443.

Goldstein, H. and Thomas, S. (1995) School Effectiveness and 'Value Added' Analysis, *Forum*, Vol. 37, no. 2, pp. 36–8.

Good, T. L. and Brophy, J. (1986) Teacher Behaviour and Student Achievement in M. C. Wittrock (ed) *Handbook of Research on Teaching*, Collier Mac-Millan, London.

Gray, J. (1995) The Quality of Schooling: Frameworks for Judgement, in J. Gray and B. Wilcox (eds) *Good School, Bad School*, Open University Press, Milton Keynes.

Handy, C. (1984) *Taken for Granted? Understanding Schools as Organizations*, Schools Council/Longman, York.

Handy, C. (1997) Schools for Life and Work, in *Living Education: Essays in honour of John Tomlinson*, Paul Chapman, London.

Hargreaves, D. and Hopkins, D. (1991) *The Empowered School: The Management and Practice of Development Planning*, Cassell, London.

Harlen, W. and James, M. (1996) *Assessment and Learning*. Unpublished paper prepared for the BERA Policy Task Group on Assessment.

Head, J. (1996) Gender Identity and Cognitive Style, in P. Murphy, and C. Gipps, *Equity in the Classroom. Towards an Effective Pedagogy for Girls and Boys*, Falmer/Unesco Publishing.

Hirst, P. (1974) *Knowledge and the Curriculum: A collection of philosophical Papers*, Routledge and Kegan Paul, London.

Hopewell, B. (1996) Book Review of McMaster, M. (1995) The Intelligence Advantage – organizing for complexity, *Long Range Planning*, Vol. 29, no. 6, pp. 902–4.

Hopkins, D. (1989) *Evaluation for School Development*, Open University Press, Milton Keynes.

Hopkins, D., Ainscow, M. and West, M. (1994) *School Improvement in an Era of Change*, Cassell, London.

Huberman, M. (1988) Teachers' Careers and School Improvement, *Journal of Curriculum Studies 20*, Vol. 2, pp. 119–32.

ILEA (1984) *Improving Secondary Schools*, ILEA, London.

Inspection Report No. 100489, Christ Church C/E School.

Joyce, B. (1991) The Doors to School Improvement, *Educational Leadership*, Vol. 48, no. 8, pp. 59–62.

Joyce, B. and Showers, B. (1988) *Student Achievement through Staff Development*, Longman, New York.

Joyce, B., Calhoun, E. and Hopkins, D. (1997) *Models of Learning – Tools for Teaching*, Open University Press, Buckingham.

Licht, B. G. and Dweck, C. (1983) Sex Differences in Achievement Orientations: Consequences for Academic Choices and Attainments, in M. Marland (ed), *Sex Differentiation and Schooling*, Heinemann Educational Books, London.

Lightfoot, S. L. (1983) *The Good High School: Portraits of Character and Culture*, Basic Books, New York.

Louis, K. S. and Miles, M. B. (1992) *Improving the Urban High School: What Works and Why*, Cassell, London.

MacBeath, J. (1997, forthcoming) *Learning to Achieve: Evaluating Study Support*, The Prince's Trust, London.

MacBeath, J., Thomson, B., Arrowsmith, J. and Forbes, D. (1992) *Using Ethos Indicators in Secondary School Self-Evaluation: Taking Account of the Views of Pupils, Parents and Teachers*, HM Inspectors of Schools, The Scottish Office Education Department.

MacGilchrist, B. (1996) Linking Staff Development with Children's Learning, *Educational Leadership*, Vol. 53, no. 6, pp. 72–5.

MacGilchrist, B., Mortimore, P., Savage, J. and Beresford, C. (1995) *Planning Matters*, Paul Chapman, London.

Mayo, E. (1930) Changing methods in industry, *Personnel Journal*, no. 8.

McMahon, A. (1993) *Action Research for School Managers: a Distance Learning Module*, University of Bristol.

McMaster, M. (1995) *The Intelligent Advantage: Organising for Complexity*, Knowledge Based Development Co. Ltd.

Mortimore, P. (1991) The Nature and Findings of Research on School Effectiveness in the Primary Sector, in S. Riddell and S. Brown (eds) *School Effectiveness Research: Its Messages for School Improvement*, HMSO, Edinburgh.

Mortimore, P. (1993) School Effectiveness and the Management of Effective Learning and Teaching, *School Effectiveness and School Improvement*, Vol. 4, no. 4, pp. 290–310.

Mortimore, P. (1996) *School Effectiveness and School Improvement: Issues Facing Senior Managers in Primary and Secondary Schools*, Oldham Education Department Quality Development Service Seminar Series, June.

Mortimore, P. and Mortimore, J. (eds) (1991) *The Primary Head: Roles, Responsibilities and Reflections*, Paul Chapman, London.

Mortimore, P., Sammons, P. and Thomas, S. (1994) School Effectiveness and Value Added Measures, *Assessment in Education: Principles, Policy and Practice*, Vol. 1, no. 3, pp. 315–22.

Mortimore, P., Sammons, P., Stoll, L., Lewis, D. and Ecob, R. (1988) *School Matters: The Junior Years*, Paul Chapman, London.

Murphy, P. (1988) Gender and Assessment, *Curriculum,* Vol. 9, no. 3, Winter.

Myers, K. (1980) Sex Stereotyping at Option Choice, MA dissertation, Institute of Education, University of London.

Myers, K. (1992) *Genderwatch! After the Education Reform Act,* Cambridge University Press.

Myers, K. (1995) *School Improvement in Action: A Critical History of a School Improvement Project,* EdD Dissertation, University of Bristol.

Myers, K. (1996a) Private report.

Myers, K. (1996b) This Head of English Turned Her Department Round. How did She Do It? *TES School Management Update,* 29 November, p. 6.

Myers, K. (ed) (1996c) *School Improvement in Practice: Schools Make a Difference Project,* Falmer Press.

Nias, J., Southworth, G. and Yeomans, R. (1989) *Staff Relationships in the Primary School: A Study of Organizational Cultures,* Cassell, London.

Nias, J., Southworth, G., and Campbell, P. (1992) *Whole School Curriculum Development in the Primary School,* Falmer Press, London.

NUT/University of Strathclyde (1995) *Schools Speak for Themselves – Towards a Framework for Self Evaluation.*

Nuttall, D. (1986) *Actual and Predicted Performance Scores by Ethnic Group,* Schools Research & Statistics Branch, ILEA.

O'Donaghue, C., Thomas, S., Goldstein, H. and Knight, T. (1997) *DfEE Study of Value Added to 16–18 Year Olds in England,* Department for Education and Employment, London.

Ofsted (1995) *Planning Improvement: Schools Post-Inspection Action Plans,* HMSO, London.

Perkins, D. (1995) *Outsmarting IQ: The Emergence of Learnable Intelligence,* Free Press, New York.

Peters, T. and Waterman, R. (1982) *In Search of Excellence,* Harper & Row, London.

Piaget, J. (1932) *The Language and Thought of the Child,* 2nd edition, New York.

Powell, M. (1980) The Beginning Teacher Evaluation Study: a Brief History of a Major Research Project, in C. Denham and A. Lieberman (eds) *Time to Learn,* National Institute of Education, Washington DC.

Reynolds, D., Hopkins, D. and Stoll, L. (1993) Linking School Effectiveness Knowledge and School Improvement Practice: Towards a Synergy, *School Effectiveness and School Improvement,* Vol. 4, no. 1, pp. 37–58.

Reynolds, D., Bollen, R., Creemers, B., Hopkins, D., Stoll, L. and Lagerweij, N. (1996) *Making Good Schools: Linking School Effectiveness and School Improvement,* Routledge, London.

Riley, J. (1996) *The Teaching of Reading: The Development of Literacy in the Early Years of School,* Paul Chapman, London.

Robertson, P. and Sammons, P. (1997) Improving School Effectiveness: A Project in Progress. Paper presented at the Tenth International Congress for School Effectiveness and Improvement, Memphis, Tennessee.

Rogers, C. (1982) *Education – a Personal Activity,* Pavic Publications, Sheffield Polytechnic.

Rosenholtz, S. (1989) *Teachers' Workplace: The Social Organization of Schools*, Longman, New York.

Rosenthal, R. and Jacobson, L. (1968) *Pygmalion in the Classroom*, Holt, Rinehart & Winston, New York.

Rudduck, J., Chaplain, R. and Wallace, G. (1996) *School Improvement. What Can Pupils Tell Us?* David Fulton, London.

Rutter, J., Maughan, B., Mortimore, P. and Ouston, J. (1979) *Fifteen Thousand Hours: Secondary Schools and their Effects on Children*, Paul Chapman, London.

Säljö, R. (1979) Learning about Learning, *Higher Education*, Vol. 8, pp. 443–51.

Salovey, P. and Mayer, J. D. (1990) Emotional Intelligences *Imagination, Cognition and Personality*, 9, pp. 185–211.

Sammons, P., Hillman, J. and Mortimore, P. (1995) *Key Characteristics of Effective Schools: A Review of School Effectiveness Research*. Report commissioned by the Office for Standards in Education, Institute of Education and Office for Standards in Education.

Sammons, P., Thomas, S. and Mortimore, P. (1997) *Forging Links: Effective Schools and Effective Departments*, Paul Chapman, London.

Schein, E. H. (1985) *Organizational Culture and Leadership*, Jossey-Bass, San Francisco, CA.

Schagen, I. (1997) Value Added Taxes the Statisticians, *TES*, 7 March, p. 14.

Schulman, L. (1987) Knowledge and Teaching Foundations of the New Reform, *Harvard Educational Review*, Vol. 57, no. 1, pp. 1–22.

Senge, P. M. (1993) *The Fifth Discipline: The Art and Practice of the Learning Organisation*, Century Business, London.

Sikes, P. J. (1992) Imposed Change and the Experienced Teacher, in M. Fullan and A. Hargreaves (eds) *Teacher Development and Educational Change*, Falmer Press, London.

Silcock, P. (1993) Can We Teach Effective Teaching? *Educational Review*, Vol. 45, no. 1 pp. 13–19.

Smith, A. (1996) *Accelerated Learning in the Classroom*, Framework Educational Press.

Soar, R. S. and Soar, R. M. (1979) Emotional Climate and Management, in P. Peterson and H. Walberg (eds) *Research on Teaching: Concepts, Findings and Implications*, McCutchan, Berkeley, CA.

Southworth, G. (1995) *Looking into Primary Headship: a Research Based Interpretation*, Falmer Press.

Stoll, L. and Fink, D. (1996) *Changing our Schools*, Open University Press, Milton Keynes.

Sutcliffe, J. (1997) Enter the Feel Bad Factor, *TES*, 10 January, p. 1.

Tabberer, R. (1996) *Teachers Make a Difference: A Research Perspective on Teaching and Learning in Primary Schools*, NFER.

Tannen, D. (1992) *You Just Don't Understand*, Virago, London.

Tizard, B., Blatchford, P., Burke, J., Farquhar, C. and Plewis, I. (1988) *Young Children at School in the Inner City*, Lawrence Erlbaum Associates, Hove.

TTA (1995) *Survey of Continuing Professional Development*, Research conducted for the TTA by MORI, June 1995, published by TTA.

van Velzen, W., Miles, M., Ekholm, M., Hameyer, U. and Robin, D. (1985) *Making School Improvement Work: A Conceptual Guide to Practice*, Acco Publishers, Leuven, Belgium.

Varlaam, A., Nuttall, D. L. and Walker, A. (1992) *What Makes Teachers Tick? A Survey of Teacher Morale and Motivation*, Centre for Educational Research, Clare Market Papers No. 4, LSE, London.

Vygotsky, L. (1987) *The Collected Works of L. S. Vygotsky*, Vol. 1, R. Reiber and A. Carton (eds), Plenum, London.

West, M. and Ainscow, M. (1991) *Managing School Development – A Practical Guide*, David Fulton, London.

West Sussex Education Department (1996) *Raising Achievement through Effective Development Planning*, West Sussex County Council.

Wheatley, M. J. (1992) *Leadership and the New Science: Learning About Organizations From an Orderly Universe*, Berrett-Koehler Publishers, San Francisco.

Index

Other Books of Interest on School Effectiveness

FORGING LINKS
Effective Schools and Effective Departments
Pam Sammons, Sally Thomas and Peter Mortimore

This major new study is a thought-provoking investigation of the concept of secondary school effectiveness. Based on a three-year study of secondary schools' GCSE results, *Forging Links* illustrates the complexities of judging school performance. The findings make a significant contribution to our understanding of the factors and processes which help schools and departments to enhance student progress.

1 85396 349 6   *Paperback*   264pp   1997

PLANNING MATTERS
The Impact of Development Planning in Primary Schools
Barbara MacGilchrist, Peter Mortimore, Jane Savage
and *Charles Beresford*

In recent years, development plans have become a feature of most schools and the majority of policy-makers and practitioners assume that by having such a plan a school will become more effective. But do they really make a difference? What impact does a development plan have on the management and organisation of the school, on the professional development of teachers and, most importantly, on pupils' learning in the classroom? Can the development planning process be used as a school improvement strategy or would schools be better investing their time and energy in other ways? This book seeks to answer these questions.

1 85396 267 8   *Paperback*   248pp   1995

FIFTEEN THOUSAND HOURS
Secondary Schools and their Effects on Children
Michael Rutter, Barbara Maughan, Peter Mortimore and *Janet Ouston*

What effects do schools have on children? Do those effects vary from one school to another? On average, children in the UK spend some 15,000 hours at school, yet remarkably little is known about how that experience affects their development. This book presents findings of one of the most detailed investigations of these questions ever undertaken.

1 85396 281 3   *Paperback*   288pp   1979

SCHOOL MATTERS
The Junior Years
Peter Mortimore, Pamela Sammons, Louise Stoll, David Lewis and *Russell Ecob*

This book is probably the most detailed account of the primary school milieu ever undertaken. The authors traced the fortunes, over a period of four years, of 2000 pupils in 50 randomly selected London primary schools.

1 85396 302 X   *Paperback*   320pp   1988

Leaflet available with fuller details on all these books